New Economy Edge

The New Economy Excellence Series

New Economy Edge:
Strategies and Techniques for Boosting Online Profitability

Jeremy Kourdi,

Senior Vice President and Director, The Economist Conferences

JOHN WILEY & SONS, LTD

Chichester ● New York ● Weinheim ● Brisbane ● Singapore ● Toronto

Other Wiley Editorial Offices

John Wiley & Sons, Inc., 605 Third Avenue,
New York, NY 10158-0012, USA

WILEY-VCH Verlag GmbH, Pappelallee 3,
D-69469 Weinheim, Germany

John Wiley & Sons, Australia Ltd, 33 Park Road, Milton,
Queensland 4064, Australia

John Wiley & Sons (Asia) Pte Ltd, 2 Clementi Loop #02-01,
Jin Xing Distripark, Singapore 129809

John Wiley & Sons (Canada) Ltd, 22 Worcester Road,
Rexdale, Ontario M9W 1L1, Canada

British Library Cataloguing in Publication Data

A catalogue record for this book is available from the British Library

ISBN 0-471-49844-0

Typeset in 11/14pt Garamond by Mayhew Typesetting, Rhayader, Powys

This book is printed on acid-free paper responsibly manufactured from
sustainable forestry, in which at least two trees are planted for each
one used for paper production.

CONTENTS

ACKNOWLEDGEMENTS

This book is the result of the support and encouragement of many people, and while the execution, style and shortcomings are my own, their expertise and help must certainly be acknowledged. First, my excellent editor at John Wiley & Sons, John Moseley, and his talented colleagues whose patience and energy are much appreciated and who have been a valuable source of advice and well-informed opinion. Second, my friends and many colleagues at The Economist Group who have, without doubt, provided the most intelligent, stimulating and innovative environment in which to work, learn and develop.

Finally, my gratitude goes, as always, to my wife Julie, my son Thomas and my daughter Louise, who have not only provided constant support and encouragement, but also thought-provoking opinions and the inspiration to write.

Reports of the power of the internet – for businesses, customers and consumers – have swung violently in nature during the past decade. Some people claim that the 'new economy' is the greatest force since the onset of the Industrial Revolution, while others argue that this is hype, pointing to inflated share prices and business failures as examples of their case. The truth is that the greatest business tool of all remains unchallenged. Without wishing to sound romantic or philosophical it is, quite simply put, the *human spirit*. The ability to serve customers, innovate, compete, lead and deliver all of the other entrepreneurial qualities is what matters, and in the early twenty-first century the key to achieving these things, delivering competitive advantage and driving profitability, is mastery of the Internet. This is the commercial *Edge* that is the title – and focus – for this business book.

There has been a sense among senior executives that commercial online developments can be hugely disruptive and expensive; that somehow, because of its innate complexity, risk, newness and idiosyncrasies, the Internet needs to be focused on separately and in isolation from other, more traditional profit-generating activities. Focusing on e-commerce activities separately to other commercial strategies and tactics is a terribly flawed approach: it fails to recognise the all-pervading benefits, and risks, of the Internet, and it is now very difficult to sustain for any size of business over any period of time. On the other hand, the Internet has been referred to as simply the latest business tool, analogous to the telephone. A business would not have

Table 1: Worldwide growth of the Internet

Internet users (millions)	1998	2001	% change
USA	51.8	107.4	107
Europe	23.2	55.5	139
Asia	8.1	22.5	178
Japan	9.0	18.3	103
Rest of world	9.0	27.8	209

(Source: International Data Corporation)

a telephone strategy, so the argument goes, so why should it develop an e-commerce strategy? I have marginally more sympathy with this approach, but it is flawed nevertheless. The Internet is much more than a simple business tool, *the Internet fundamentally changes what customers want, expect and can have.* It is a major source of competitive advantage for reducing cost, driving revenue, innovating and – across a whole range of business measures – adding value for customers.

The truth and reality, therefore, lie between the two competing views. The Internet's reach and potential continue to grow (see Table 1) and, because of its scope and dynamic change, an online strategy needs to be integrated into the overall business much more than *ever before.* The Internet is just too significant a driver of growth and profit to be ignored or not fully integrated into the overall business. The current economic slowdown, possibly leading to a recession, merely serves to emphasise the importance of mastery of the Internet as a source of greater commercial efficiency and competitiveness.

This book focuses on practical strategies and techniques for driving profitability, and includes online activities providing a whole range of innovative tactics, ideas and opportunities that are fully integrated into the business. To a large extent, it assumes that the reader is a senior business manager who is keen to drive profits and develop the commercial potential of their business through online activities. In addition, however, the book is also relevant to all managers, whatever level of development and awareness they may have of e-commerce and Internet-related issues and at whatever stage of development and expertise their business has reached. This is because it provides *practical* ideas and techniques for maximising revenue and reducing costs, both within a business operation that is already established and by implementing and developing new online activities where the stage of development is less advanced.

Distinctions are often drawn between business to consumer (B2C) and business to business (B2B) applications of the Internet, but in this book no distinction is intended. Much of the book emphasises techniques for increasing profitability in a business facing the consumer or end-user, but it is important to recognise that in the new economy *every customer is a consumer*, whatever the organisation. Above all else, the Internet delivers discontinuity, innovation and new ways of thinking about the world. In addition, it is simultaneously a mass medium (like television) and a personal, one-to-one medium (like direct mail). I believe that these two attributes blur the traditional concepts of b2c and b2b. My belief is that they were nothing more than shorthand for describing certain attributes – and providing a measure of focus in the early days of the new economy – for businesses that were trying to come to terms with the impact of the Internet. This book and its concepts, including customer focus, knowledge management, cost reduction, brand building and innovation, are therefore relevant to any commercial operation wishing to improve profitability by using online business techniques.

The ideas and examples in the book are readily applicable and are designed to stimulate further thoughts, leading to the development of a clear action plan. Examples range from how to make savings using online purchasing and procurement to reducing risks and costs by researching online, developing customer relationship management and devising new sources of revenue. In effect, the book will *enable* business managers to use the power of the Internet to become exceptional, enhancing profitability and improving competitiveness and overall performance.

The benefits of this book

This book is fundamentally focused on helping managers create and sustain competitive advantage using the Internet. It will:

- provide thought-provoking guidance, analysis and examples;
- enable busy executives to develop their own strategy easily – and implement it quickly;
- outline key principles as well as leading-edge solutions to the central issue of developing competitiveness and profitability using the Internet;
- demystify the most significant e-business concepts, strategies, tools and trends driving profitability;
- be results driven – helping executives to consider the issues and master the ideas that could transform their business.

Features and symbols are an integral part of the book and include implementation checklists, diagrams, vital questions and answers and guides to getting started on a particular topic, as well as data and additional sources of further information.

Understanding the nature of online business

CHAPTER 1

Overview

This introductory chapter highlights the key trends in the on-going development of e-commerce, outlining how and where the Internet is having the greatest impact, and focusing on the seven key principles driving change for the online business that leaders must consider essential to a successful online business strategy. These themes and their practical implications are explored in greater detail in subsequent chapters.

Understanding the impact of the Internet: the seven principles driving change online

There are seven key principles driving change for the online business. These are:

1. The balance of power is shifting decisively to the customer.
2. The Internet is revolutionising sales techniques and perceptions of leading brands.

3 The pace of business activity and change is rapidly accelerating, and the need to be flexible, adaptive, customer focused and innovative is at a premium.

4 Competition in all its forms is intensifying.

5 Managing and leveraging knowledge is a key skill – and knowledge is a key strategic resource that needs to be nurtured and developed.

6 Companies are transforming themselves into extended enterprises in order to add value for their customers. They are re-evaluating factors as fundamental as their objectives, markets and competencies.

7 The Internet is increasing interactivity among people, companies and industries.

1 The balance of power is shifting decisively to the customer

This agent of change has two elements: first, customers are now not only much freer to choose from a global market but also more demanding in their expectations for service. Second, e-commerce offers customers information richness and reach at the same time.

E-commerce blurs the traditional business trade-off between reaching large sections of customers with limited information, or small segments of customers with rich amounts of information. The Internet can often provide both, and this allows marketing and sales strategies to be redefined, taking advantage of the unique closeness of many current and potential customers through a one-to-one medium.

Until the advent of the Internet and the Web, this trade-off was clear, manifest in the ways that companies advertised their products and services. For companies wanting to reach millions of customers, mass-market techniques such as television advertising provided opportunities to communicate information content, brand identity and emotion in a concise but shallow message. TV and print advertising offered reach, but very limited richness. Alternatively (and it was an alternative), if a company wanted to share a great deal of value-adding information with customers, it had to target them carefully, limiting the numbers to be reached and ensuring that these customers were the core market.

Using the Internet, companies can efficiently personalise their information richness to as broad or as narrow a segment of customers as they wish. Classic sales strategies can be redefined to take advantage of the unique properties of the Internet, so that every customer is only a click away from the company. This issue is explored further in Chapter 4, Developing your markets to increase profitability.

2 The Internet is revolutionising sales techniques and perceptions of leading brands

Getting people to buy online is a massive new area of activity. It is important to note, however, that at the start of the twenty-first century it is the trend and potential for increased business online that are enormous, not the absolute level of business itself (although there are significant fluctuations between industries). This book argues that online business is a key driver of profitability and competitive advantage now and in the future, and it is the *trend* that is set to continue growing.

Three factors stand out as being vitally important to online selling: the concept of *brand personality*, the importance of *customer loyalty*, and the value of *data mining*.

Brand personality

The Internet enables businesses to amplify the unique, competitive characteristics of their organisation and products – their brands. This has two significant implications: first, to succeed, businesses need to use the Internet in a way that drives value for the customer and is commensurate with their market. For example, offering pensions policies online requires an approach different to that needed for selling teenage computer games online, because the nature of the market is different. Second, the Internet amplifies the brand so that it reaches a global market. This requires much, much more than simply setting up a web site; involving money, people and closeness to the market, but it is feasible nonetheless. Conversely, the online environment also exposes weak brands, and these can be damaged swiftly and decisively when mistakes are made, as customers can perceive weaknesses more quickly and shift to competitors much more easily than ever before.

Customer loyalty

As a result of customers' ability to move to competitors – the fact that the balance of power is shifting so decisively to the customer – competitive advantage online comes to those businesses that fight to retain their customers. This requires constant renewal, an approach that actively seeks out innovations and new sources of value for the customer.

Data mining

Data mining is the process of acquiring, analysing, storing and using customer-focused information. It is a key source of competitive advantage and profit growth, and it represents one of the Internet's most significant benefits to businesses. Web sites now can capture massive amounts of data on each individual customer – even though there may be thousands of customers – and this can be used to add value to the customer relationship, driving every aspect of the organisation's development from sales strategies to new products. This important concept and how it can be used in practice is also outlined in greater detail in Chapter 4, Developing your markets to increase profitability.

3 The pace of business activity and change is rapidly accelerating, and the need to be flexible, adaptive, customer focused and innovative is at a premium

While Internet time signifies many things to different people, one leading feature is that the Internet is experienced in the present: every day, any time, 24/7 (24 hours a day, 7 days a week), local and global at the same time. Across time zones, geography and business activities, Internet time is always *now*. Business activity on the Internet is always happening: opportunities are won and lost minute to minute, globally.

KEY CONCEPT

The Internet adds a new perception of business time: 24/7, where developments take place online 24 hours a day, seven days a week.

Internet time introduces a new perception of business time as always 'on', urgent and demanding a rapid response. The challenge for managers is to reconcile their business and their own personal perceptions of time with the perceived reality of Internet time.

In addition, the Internet compresses time and action into shorter and shorter intervals. Since change occurs simultaneously with actions taken on the Internet, everything is urgent. Feedback on actions taken or comments made online comes immediately, from anyone logged on to the Internet. Once a company is online it participates in a world of unrelenting urgency, where business strategy and action are compressed into today's activities and the pressure to participate is always high.

The three key drivers of change resulting from Internet time are, first, that the Internet is always available and working. Second, time and action are compressed, there is a culture of urgency and the ability for feedback to be swift, if not immediate. Third, the result of this Internet immediacy is that managers need to respond to important and 'trivial' issues quickly, as something trivial on the Internet can be rapidly amplified and distorted into something much larger!

Internet time requires managers to respond rapidly to both the important and the trivial simultaneously. If business activities are always in real time and urgent, then distinguishing between what is important and what is trivial is a particular skill that is best developed soon. Dissatisfied customers online do not complain to a few people about your company; they complain to potentially millions of consumers though chat rooms, bulletin boards and their own web sites. Similarly, competition on the Web is fast and observable. One company's innovation on the Web is its competitors' chance to copy or counter it quickly. The strategies of companies on the Web are transparent to their customers and competitors alike.

4 Competition in all its forms is intensifying

The nature of the online environment means that competition is intensifying between similar businesses, suppliers, customers, new entrants and businesses that can substitute for each other. This is true for 'traditional' offline businesses, highlighting the need for every business to embrace the Internet and to develop online capabilities as a source of competitive advantage. Practical techniques for competing online are examined in Chapter 12, Resource building: the key to the competitive online business. The real key to being competitive and driving profits in the face of change and rivalry is to stay close to the market and, following on from this, to develop key strategic resources. These should provide advantages that are unique or, at the very least, difficult to replicate.

One of the consequences of this increase in competition is the fact that pricing online is significantly different to traditional pricing methods offline. Because this one issue has such an impact on other factors such as customer loyalty, market share, brand perception and profitability as a whole, it is reviewed in further detail in its own chapter (Chapter 5, Internet pricing). It is worth mentioning here that two forces affect pricing on the Internet: *transaction costs*, which can be significantly lower than for other channels, and *price transparency*, where price differentials (usually between different territories) for the same product or service are exposed. The dual impact of these two factors means that traditional pricing strategies become undermined by e-commerce. The situation therefore becomes one of innovating using price, or risking being undermined by it. This issue is explored further in Chapter 7, Building brands and customer loyalty.

5 Managing and leveraging knowledge is a key skill – and knowledge is a key strategic resource that needs to be nurtured and developed

Knowledge is at a premium for the profitable online business. Those that succeed are knowledge rich: they value the information they have, they actively seek and manage the information they need, and they ensure that all sources of knowledge and information – from people employed in the organisation to customers 'outside' the business – are nurtured, respected and kept informed. Practical techniques for managing knowledge to enhance profitability are explored in detail in Chapter 10.

For managers in established companies in many service and manufacturing industries, the cycle of Internet learning in relation to products and services is foreign to the way they normally consider designing, releasing and improving their products. In their minds, being first to market is always good. Version management is fine, but versions must be well planned and tested thoroughly before release. Product strategies must

KEY CONCEPT

Internet business learning is continuous, evolutionary and rapid. Because of this, the most successful online businesses are those that have developed an open, dynamic and flexible approach.

be clearly formulated before products are designed and released to the market. Companies should design products to be right the first time. These accepted principles of product innovation in established companies are now being actively violated, not only in the IT industry with PCs, printers and cell phones, but also in more traditional industries such as automobiles, insurance, banking and retailing. It is in these 'established' industries where 'Internet learning' is influencing the cycle of product design, release and testing – try it, revise it and, most of all, do it rapidly!

Case Study: Using the Internet to develop knowledge ('learning by doing')

The metaphor for learning and innovation on the Internet is the process of designing, releasing and improving software in the IT industry. Software products like Microsoft Windows tend never to be developed with 100 per cent of the features and quality required by customers, launched into the market until the product cycle matures, and then either withdrawn or redesigned from the bottom up to be launched again or replaced

CONTINUED . . . Case Study: Using the Internet to develop knowledge ('learning by doing')

some years in the future. Instead, software is developed, launched *and continuously improved*. If the commercial proposition is right, customers will be pleased – and may prefer – to go along with this approach, knowing that they will benefit from an on-going improvement process.

The standard product design, release and sell cycle applicable to cars, insurance, banking, consumer goods and industrial products does not apply to software. In the future, the standard cycle will apply in fewer and fewer areas, as the Internet provides:

- instant customer feedback on desired product features and enhancements;
- feedback on how effectively the desired features have been executed or delivered;
- the opportunity to sell to customers once, a product that will continually be updated or enhanced, adding value for the customer and enhancing future cash flows for the business;
- the ability to take advantage of cost reductions either to reduce prices or to increase margins.

Of course, there are many other benefits, usually depending on the nature of the industry. Software features are continuously tested in the marketplace with groups of customers, and software products are released with known quality defects or 'bugs', since companies want to be first in the market with their products. They assume that bugs will be corrected in later versions. Software companies aim for modular releases of their products rather than grand designs, since customer

> **CONTINUED ... Case Study: Using the Internet to develop knowledge ('learning by doing')**
>
> acceptance of the product is always uncertain until the product is used. Thus, learning and doing in the software industry are compressed into single acts that evolve continuously with customer interactions and competitor responses. From a quality perspective, products are never perfect. With new products and new versions of established products, being first to market is critical.

Because the nature of the Internet is one of continuous, sustained and fast evolution, it makes little sense to wait and perfect ideas. The opportunity — and expectation — exists to launch, test and perfect products and services using the Internet, and this can be a powerful method of building customer loyalty, innovation and advantage.

6 Companies are transforming themselves into extended enterprises in order to add value for their customers. They are re-evaluating factors as fundamental as their objectives, markets and competencies

The content (what is sold), the context (where and when it is sold) and the infrastructure of the business can be fundamentally redefined using e-commerce, with massive repercussions for the strategy of the business and its operations. The example of Amazon.com highlights the changes that can blast through an industry like book selling, but other industries normally regarded as conservative and traditional — such as retail banking — are also being redefined. A valuable place to start is therefore with the fundamentals of the business: identifying and creating new opportunities, as well as removing and destroying old practices that only existed because the Internet was not there yet! Online, it is possible to reconfigure the content, market and infrastructure of the business so that the accepted model of the company and the industry is completely redefined. This issue is explored in further detail in Chapter 8, Using the Internet for profitable product innovation, and Chapter 9, Suppliers and supply chains: reducing costs and adding value.

The Internet is driving an on-going process of creative construction and destruction of commercial business models. As new business models based on the Internet and the Web develop around the world, this process of creative destruction and construction will continue to challenge businesses and whole industries. The key for managers in established companies is to *anticipate* the forms of creative destruction that are likely to occur in their industries. Then they have to begin reconfiguring their value chains to take advantage of these changes before new entrants displace them.

Case Study: The power of the Internet to redefine entire industries

An example of an industry being fundamentally redefined is the retail banking industry. Here, the evolution of an integrated business model dependent on a mix of factors, including branch offices that promote products and direct channels of ATM, phone and Internet banking, has been changed by a new model that reconfigures the content, context and infrastructure of banking and financial services. Over the last decade, bankers worked hard to develop alternative direct channels through ATMs, phone and Internet banking that would give their customers access to bank services at lower transaction costs to the bank. Progressive bank managers focused on lowering

CONTINUED . . . Case Study: The power of the Internet to redefine entire industries

the costs of banking, increasing direct services and developing their branches into sales and service centres.

Today, however, the content, context and infrastructure of banking are under threat from companies like Intuit. Intuit offers millions of higher-income households the possibility of linking directly to banks, insurance companies and asset management firms over the Internet, selecting their financial service providers as needed, without any inertia or reason to stay with the last financial service provider. Instead of being locked into the products and delivery channels of a particular bank, customers can choose from a broad array of financial service providers from their home or office PC. All they have to do is use Quicken software as the window to the world of financial services.

This emerging model of retail banking threatens the integrated model in three ways.

- Intuit, through its Quicken software, becomes the new intermediary with customers rather than the banks directly. The banks become product suppliers.
- The new model appeals to higher-income segments of customers, leaving lower-margin customers to traditional banks.
- Industry changes such as deregulation, combined with changes driven by the Internet (and technology), mean that access to banking, insurance and other forms of financial services will be available to customers online, through programs such as Quicken and through partnering arrangements between firms like Intuit and financial service providers.

7   The Internet is increasing interactivity among people, companies and industries

For any communications network, the number of nodes (N) on a network yields that number squared in potential value (N^2) to users.[1]

This view, put forward by Robert Metcalf and known as Metcalf's Law, highlights the fact that the millions of people using the Internet have created (and will continue to create) the conditions for massive increases in the value of the Internet to people and firms. This is shown by the resulting meteoric growth in the number of people using phone and email networks, and the fact that many is better than few. It is the case that the more the Internet is used, the greater the value of using it and so the more it will be used. Through the interactions that it enables, it is now creating human and business value of tremendous proportions.

Interactions, defined as the searching, co-ordinating and monitoring that people do when they exchange goods, services and ideas, increase when the number of users passes a critical mass. Clearly, this mass has been exceeded with the Internet, resulting in exceptional potential value. Often, all that is required is the belief that the opportunity to innovate using the Internet exists and a commitment to it, although for many managers, particularly in traditional businesses, this is difficult to achieve. In addition, the Internet is driving a culture change in business globally, with the emphasis on 'can do' flexibility and an approach emphasising the need to 'just do it'.

Harnessing the seven principles driving change online

Central to success in growing and developing profits from online business activities are the *ten critical drivers of e-commerce success*. These are outlined in detail in the next chapter, but their importance is such that they are best introduced as early as possible! They are the need to focus on:

1 developing the *content* of online initiatives;
2 effective and appropriate *communication*;
3 ensuring that *customer care* and loyalty are developed as a priority;
4 understanding the benefits and potential pitfalls of establishing *community and culture* for the online business;
5 delivering *convenience and ease* for customers;
6 understanding the importance and value of *connectivity*, both with other sites and with users;
7 financial drivers of *cost and profitability* online;
8 practical techniques for *customisation* – building an irresistible offer that exactly matches each customer's needs;
9 developing resources that increase the business's online *capability*, ensuring that it is dynamic, responsive and flexible;
10 an approach that maintains *competitiveness*.

Understanding the seven principles of e-commerce clearly helps to outline the challenges in developing a successful e-commerce strategy. Responding to these seven principles and developing an effective, profit-driven approach to e-commerce involves taking action on a wide range of fronts, and this is explored further in Chapter 2, Focusing the profit-driven online business.

Focusing the profit-driven online business

Overview

This chapter is concerned with organising your business to maximise profitability. It will enable you to create and develop profitable e-commerce activities by helping you to understand the effect of the Internet on employees, markets, customers and business partners. Key issues covered include:

- Reviewing whether products or services are suitable for e-commerce, and if so, *why* – what features make them distinctive and successful?
- Understanding how to focus your business so that it is driven by customer needs, not product issues. A framework for developing a successful e-business is outlined, focusing on the ten critical drivers of online success.

Assessing the e-commerce potential of your products and services

The first step in focusing your online activities and deriving maximum benefit is to understand what the main advantages

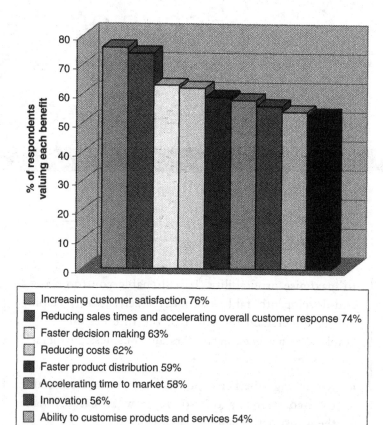

The following benefits are listed in the chart legend:

- Increasing customer satisfaction 76%
- Reducing sales times and accelerating overall customer response 74%
- Faster decision making 63%
- Reducing costs 62%
- Faster product distribution 59%
- Accelerating time to market 58%
- Innovation 56%
- Ability to customise products and services 54%
- Globalisation 53%

Figure 2.1: Key business benefits of the Internet

Source: Aggregation of information from the EIU and other online information sources[2] (January 2001)

are for your organisation. Recent research conducted across a broad range of businesses highlights some of the key benefits (see Figure 2.1).

The customer as driver of profits: online, offline and always

The key element here is to understand your customers' views of what makes your products distinctive and successful. Of course, this is not new, but only by clearly understanding this is it possible to determine whether your goods are suitable for sale over the Internet, and how best to realise the opportunities. It can be helpful to research your customers' views when assessing the business benefits of the Internet for your organisation and their impact on your customers.

 Vital questions and answers

. . . when considering selling products or services via the Internet

1 Is your product or company well recognised?

If your product or company is an established brand name, that will usually provide the trust and security needed for potential customers to buy from you over the Internet. If not, additional measures and incentives may be required to ensure that potential Internet customers feel secure.

The key issue here is whether your brand is well known and your product easily recognised: if so, no problem, that will provide the level of understanding and security that people need. If not, then additional measures to provide customers with reassurance that they are buying from a reputable business may include:

■ Customer *testimonials*, press cuttings and reviews, a client list and possibly references or agents where the product can be discussed or viewed.

CONTINUED ... **Vital questions and answers**

■ *Trial packages and offers*, money-back guarantees and financial incentives to buy may also encourage customers to try the product or service.

■ *An offline publicity campaign* that successfully establishes the brand and product among its target audience and also drives traffic to the site.

However, there is an important warning here for the profit-focused business, and that is the need to manage cash flows carefully. Many new and energetic businesses tend to forget this rather mundane rule, and Internet-focused enterprises are newer and more energetic than most! The short history of the new economy is already littered with examples of businesses that promised much and invested even more to establish their brands, but in the end spent too much, or at least, *too much too soon*.

2 Is it feasible for you to sell your product or service directly to consumers and businesses from your web site?

The issue of feasibility encompasses a range of issues, including:

■ Is it *legal* to sell services online? If so, your site can be used to sell and deliver the product. If not, it may be used for more traditional marketing (e.g. providing product information and directing customers to distributors or sales outlets), as well as adding value to your value proposition with customer support and service.

CONTINUED . . . Vital questions and answers

■ How *convenient* is it for customers to buy online? If your product or service can conveniently be sold online (e.g. books, music or airline tickets), online purchasing needs to drive the site. If your product cannot easily be sold online (e.g. cars, houses or legal services), your priorities may either be enhancing your value proposition (e.g. by enhancing customer service) or driving traffic to other sales outlets and distributors where the sale can be completed – or both.

■ Are there *physical limitations* on the product or service you provide? This may arise if you need people to install a product or deliver a service in person (e.g. lawyers). If the answer is yes, you can still focus the site on online purchasing, but it may be necessary to limit or define your service in terms of area (or zip or postal code). If there are no physical limitations, your site is probably suited to online purchasing.

3   Can you clearly identify and reach the target market for your product or service?

This question has two key elements: identifying and then reaching target markets.

■ *Identifying customers* – if you can clearly identify the psychographic profile of potential customers (the combination of psychological and demographic factors that will drive them to buy), this information needs to drive the look, feel and 'culture' of the site. For example, a web site selling outdoor sporting goods will probably need a wholly different feel to one that is

CONTINUED ... Vital questions and answers

selling financial services. This is not simply because the products are different, but because the likely mindset and priorities of the customers (who may actually be the same people, at different times, for both businesses) will differ. If you cannot clearly identify the target market, market research leading to clear market segmentation is necessary. If your market segment is large (for example, an online travel agency), the most effective way forward online is still to follow a segmentation approach, speaking to the needs of each customer group (and ideally each individual customer) as closely as possible. In the case of the online travel agency, this may mean dividing the site into different types of holiday based on types of customer, such as adventure holidays, beach holidays, city breaks, or possibly by age (18–30, young families, 50+) and so forth.

■ *Reaching customers* – it may be entirely feasible to identify customers and convince them to buy, but the sale needs to be completed off-line, usually via a distribution outlet. Understanding how best to reach and service customers in a manner that is easy and in line with the customers' wishes can often require research, process planning and investment. One example of this would be a site for a film

KEY CONCEPT

One of the greatest potential dangers of online selling is assuming that your customers will want to buy in one way, perhaps the same way in which they have always bought. The Internet enables customers to have a much greater amount of freedom, convenience and autonomy. Frequently, the business that recognises this best and constructs its web site accordingly – possibly going as far as inventing an entirely new commmercial model – receives the greatest competitive advantage.

CONTINUED . . . **Vital questions and answers**

company: they can convince you to go to the movies, they can even sell you a ticket, but to get the product you need to go to a cinema! A less obvious example is a company launching a new computer games console: some customers may be adult (and hence have the authority to buy), some may be children needing to persuade others to buy it for them. Some may be prepared to buy online using a credit card, some may prefer to visit a distribution outlet to view the product. The site therefore needs to be built so that it is flexible enough to recognise all of these customer options, and positively embrace them as a source of competitive advantage.

4   Can you use your site to add value to your customer relationships?

It is important that the web site does not simply replicate existing sales methods, using an existing sales model transferred to the Internet, but that it employes the online medium to generate value for the customer and new business opportunities for the vendor. For example, if you are managing an international conference business, the challenges you face are not simply selling delegate registrations online, but also ensuring that the web site is used to attract *new* customers and increase *repeat* business, both by traditional promotions but also by adding value to customer relationships. However, there are a range of virtual conferences and other electronic products that can also be developed, sold and delivered electronically: a whole new business model, an entirely new opportunity grown out of existing activities and resources.

CONTINUED . . . Vital questions and answers

5 How might you use your site to shield your business from potential competitive pressures?

To ensure that maximum value is derived from the web site, it is essential that it is used to counter competitive pressures, whatever their source. Potential sources of competition include other firms in your industry selling comparable products; firms within your industry selling substitute products; firms in other industries selling substitute products; and possibly even entirely new industries that are enabled as a result of technological changes. While the Internet makes competitors' actions more transparent, actually monitoring and managing the competitive situation – always a complex process – can be rendered fearsomely complex in the fast-moving, global environment of e-commerce.

Some principles to help guide your competitive strategy so that you use your web site for competitive advantage include:

- *Engaging your customers in dialogue* – not only to keep in step with their evolving needs and expectations, but also as a means of staying in touch with market developments (of course, executed correctly this is also the key to enhancing customer loyalty).
- *Building a web site that is constantly updated and has the capability to evolve its structure* – this may mean adding new sections and links, and even providing genuinely new product offers.
- *Recognising when a new business model is possible – and essential.* The Internet is rife with successful businesses that have stolen the clothes of venerable,

---

CONTINUED . . . **Vital questions and answers**

established and often more traditional businesses that
have simply taken their existing business model
online in the belief that 'if it ain't broke, don't fix it'.
The truth is that the Internet has almost certainly
broken the business model, or given your competitors the potential to break it. So start deciding how
to fix it now!

■ *Establishing a culture within the business that is both alert
to competitive pressures and able to pre-empt (or at least
react) to them.* As with the previous point, business
minds can get stuck in the past just as easily as can
business models and tools. Of course, changing
culture is a notoriously difficult feat to accomplish,
requiring both top-down change and bottom-up
organisation. Immersing people in the Internet by
training and giving people access to it is a good place
to start, but also consider how your business is
structured and how you can ensure that online issues
are routinely reflected in your business processes and
decision-making activities.

Focusing on customers: ten critical drivers of e-commerce success

Understanding the ten critical drivers

With e-business, e-commerce and other Internet issues
dominating the headlines – and investment plans – of many
businesses, it is hard to know exactly what issues are
important and what are not. The next wave of e-business
activity is likely to be characterised by a corporate

restructuring across industries and markets, as businesses either collapse, having miscalculated the key issues at which they need to succeed, or else come to dominate markets and acquire other businesses. Understanding what makes an e-business profitable is therefore a fundamental prerequisite to success.

I believe that there are ten critical issues that need to be addressed to develop a profitable e-business. These are:

1. Content.
2. Communication.
3. Customer care.
4. Community and culture.
5. Convenience and ease.
6. Connectivity (connecting with other sites and connecting with users).
7. Cost and profitability.
8. Customisation (efficient personalisation).
9. Capability (dynamic, responsive and flexible).
10. Competitiveness.

KEY CONCEPT

There are ten issues that are the key drivers of success for the profit-driven e-business, ten key dimensions along which the business's progress and effectiveness can be judged. All of these are clearly focused on meeting the customer's needs in a way that is not only dynamic and attractive, but also flexible for the business and customer. The outcome is to drive revenues while also potentially reducing costs. However, the importance of each factor varies significantly, depending on the size and maturity of the organisation.

Each of these ten factors exerts a significant – often decisive – impact on the success of an organisation's e-business activities. Clearly, some will be more important for an organisation than will others, depending on factors such as the business's stage of development, its brand strength, market and competitive position and so forth. Some of these factors are always important, notably issues such as capability and convenience, whereas other issues can assume a greater significance at a particular time (for example, the issue of competitiveness, while always in the background, may assume a sudden and striking importance).

The rest of this chapter focuses on the ten critical drivers, in no particular order, and concludes with key issues for you to consider when assessing your own organisation's e-business effectiveness.

1 Content – the need to develop compelling, credible and customer-focused information

On the Internet, customers and consumers want clear, compelling content: the two content issues for the e-business to focus on are therefore *what is offered?* and *is it compelling for the target audience?* Content is important because it sets the tone for the site and the organisation's online presence; indeed, it is a key driver of brand values in the online world. What you say and how you say it are both significant and online they inter-relate as never before, a key benefit and potential pitfall. Content needs to be rich, interesting, compelling and suited to the needs of the target audience. Usually, this also requires it to be original and informative, offering choice and expert insights unavailable elsewhere.

Furthermore, the message is the media: even if all of the issues mentioned above (original, informative etc.) are addressed, the content of the site could still fail unless it is presented in an entertaining, visually appealing and easy to use manner. An interesting analogy is with the early days of television when, quite simply, television programmes were 'talking head' radio programmes on screen. The producers assumed that the content, which had been popular for years on the radio, would translate to the TV screen. Sometimes it did, more often it did not, and producers had to learn how to use the media to its full effect. The same is true of the online environment.

There are many issues to consider when developing a compelling web site, but one of the most important and frequently cited is the need to control the flow of information. Web sites have the great advantage of being able to provide masses of information; however, they also have the great disadvantage of being able to provide masses of information! In other words, it is vital to ensure that visitors to the site can control the flow of information and their access to it, to make certain that they are not paralysed or confused by the available content and that they can find what they want quickly and easily. Online consumers are learning not to be patient: if a site takes too long to load they will not return, if it is over-crowded they will leave, if it is difficult to find what they want then they won't bother again.

The content of the site also drives the development of the brand in general and sales in particular. If you believe that a brand should have a dynamic personality that customers value, understand and relate to, then compelling content is the key to achieving this online. Content therefore needs to change and evolve, and involving customers in this process can be a simple way to achieve this. Examples of this are sites that provide reviews of products (e.g. books, software, films and other products), not only from the company running the site or from chosen experts but also from visitors to the site. This is one easy method of engaging the visitor's interest and constantly adding value.

When developing content for your web site, it is important that the needs of the target readership are clearly understood: what may work on one site in one environment may not translate at all to another. In fact, in my experience it is never sufficient to take offline content (such as brochures) and reproduce this verbatim online. This is analogous to taking a radio presenter reading aloud and just filming him or her for TV. The content is the same, but the execution is now no longer appropriate to the medium. Content therefore needs to be appropriate to the Internet, bearing in mind the need to:

- add value;
- stimulate and capture interest;
- entertain;
- be accessible and easy to use;
- be appropriate to the needs of the target audience;
- embody brand values and drive the development of the brand;
- use the media;
- develop sales;
- engage the customer – and ensure that the customer is impressed enough to want to return.

An example of a web site that is generally acknowledged by its customers as providing excellent content is FT.com, the online presence of the *Financial Times*. This site enables customers to select the news that they want (e.g. all sport) and have it delivered, regularly if desired, to the desktop or WAP phone. This example highlights the effectiveness of *tailoring* content, so that information presented at the front end matches individual customer profiles. If the web site can also inform and lead customers, as Amazon.com does successfully with its book recommendations based on a customer's reading tastes, this is also a potentially potent source of innovation using content.

2 Communication – the need to engage customers

Customers like to be listened to and online they want dialogue and interaction. Indeed, customers online – like customers anywhere – may want anonymity as well as being likely to resent the hard sell at times, but what they do not want is to be ignored when they *do* want attention. One of the key issues relating to content is therefore the need to engage customers, and this is one key area where content and communication overlap.

Communication online is more than ever about listening as much as it is about giving information. To achieve this it is important to do the following:

- Understand what interests and motivates customers, what they want to know and what they don't. This can be achieved quite simply by *asking* customers.

> **KEY CONCEPT**
>
> A recent survey of 50 leading e-commerce sites found the following:
>
> - 40 per cent of e-mail questions went unanswered;
> - only 16 per cent of sites followed up with a marketing offer to customers who had purchased from them in the last 30 days;
> - of these, only 2 per cent were personalised.

- Give customers the opportunity to interact and communicate, whether via e-mail, discussion groups, online questionnaires or offline meetings.
- Reply to customers, treating their questions as you would any enquiry or conversation, remembering that the online environment is essentially a one-to-one medium.
- Remember what customers tell you and use it in the future. Again this is surely no more than one would normally do when trying to establish a rapport or build a relationship!
- Understand the need to build trust and respect. Customers do not like to be spammed (i.e. to receive unwanted e-mail) and they are generally wary of giving too much personal information. This should be asked for only if it is needed or will be used for the development of the business, and if it is provided then the confidentiality and value of the data should be respected and the legal aspects of data protection taken into account.

- Respond to customers. This means responding to their actions (such as purchases) and questions, but it may also mean responding to the fact that they all seem to leave the site from the same page, for example. This can be discovered by using 'clickstream' data showing the movement of the customer around the site, and highlights the need to monitor the site and customers' attitudes and behaviours.
- Act swiftly, as putting the processes in place to allow a quick and effective response is an essential part of building an effective web site.
- Seek customers' opinions, usually in the form of online surveys, and then act on the information.

Communication via the Internet provides an unparalleled opportunity to engage your customers in your business; this can result in a massive range of benefits from enhanced sales, customer loyalty and repeat business to help with product development and information about competitors. However, there is an important warning. The real key to success is not simply communicating or providing the information, it is the ability to balance the customer's need for content and communication with their need (and the business's) to ensure that they receive the right information in the right amount, preventing information overload.

Examples of web sites that are effective communicators include ebusinessforum.com, which runs online and offline meetings that engage current and potential customers in new, developing and interesting e-business issues, and Hewlett-Packard (HP), which offers customers the opportunity to receive electronic newsletters (again combining content and communication). This approach was inspired by HP's position in the 1990s as a slumbering giant, an organisation that needed to regain market share and arrest its declining sales. The results of their revitalised approach is encapsulated in the revised slogan: hp invent.

3 Customer care – the need to provide customers with support and confidence

Customer care can, perhaps, be best thought of as components of a piece of valuable equipment. This includes routine or mundane features (such as the need to provide a variety of payment methods), more significant issues (such as responding to queries reactively or up-

> **KEY CONCEPT**
>
> A recent survey found that 62 per cent of people using the Internet believe that giving out personal information on the Internet is 'generally unsafe'. There is no reason to think that this figure will decline, and many businesses now recognise the commercial importance of ensuring that their web site is safe and secure for their customers.

selling and cross-selling products proactively) and the downright vital – ensuring that customers' security and privacy are respected and maintained.

Critical among these factors are the need to support customers and the requirement to instil confidence, and these can be achieved in the following ways:

- Manage customers in a subtle and flexible way, for example by offering a variety of delivery options.
- Ensure adequate (meaning both capable and ever-present) customer support so that consumers and businesses find online shopping and buying stress free. This may take the form of toll-free numbers, e-mail addresses, user groups and FAQ (frequently asked questions) pages. The concept of support 24 hours a day, 7 days a week, otherwise known as 24/7, has gained in prominence and recognition almost exclusively as a result of the explosion of interest in and activity on the Internet.
- Provide security and privacy for online transactions. Given that this is one of the greatest concerns about the rapid growth in recent years of online trading, the potential damage that may result from failing to ensure adequate security is immense.

The classic example of a business that has taken the issue of customer support and turned it into a major source of competitive advantage in the online environment is Federal Express. FedEx empowers its customers to find out the status and location of their packages by logging on to its web site. This provides support, confidentiality and ease of use; it is also interesting to note that it engages customers, using the medium to meet their needs.

4 Community and culture – the need for contact and interaction

People like people: they like to interact and they are essentially social beings, sharing interests and valuing what they have in common. Even in strictly business terms, people trust and respect those with common interests, and in the online world they also like to network and interact for their personal or organisational benefit. If a web site can offer these attributes it is well on the way to success, and it is worth remembering that for an increasing number of people weaned on chat rooms and discussion groups, *networking* is the killer application – the overriding benefit of the Internet.

In building online communities, it is important to bear in mind the culture of the Internet: it is dynamic, immediate, accessible, potentially reaching millions yet still speaking directly to the individual – essentially, it is exciting. It is also home to people who are obsessed with a particular issue, idea or product. Some or all of these intangible factors need to be woven into your online presence to ensure success. There are myriad ways to achieve this, and some of the most significant include:

- Provide visitors with expert information and insight unavailable elsewhere.

- Give people the opportunity to react, essentially getting them involved in the site and taking some ownership of the issues, ultimately leading to a sale or an improved experience for the customer that leads them to stay longer, return, recommend your site or simply add value for other customers.
- Ensure that information is easy to obtain, clear, accessible and preferably lively and entertaining.
- Offer the chance to meet and interact. How well you provide this is a measure of the degree to which you have embraced the Internet.

Examples of Internet sites that have successfully delivered the benefits of online interaction and community include iVillage.com, essentially an online community of communities, providing advice across a broad spectrum of issues. Most sites stick to their specific area of expertise, but this is often neither possible nor even desirable. Wireplay is a site developed by British Telecom (BT) to facilitate online gaming. Although its expertise is as a major international telecoms provider, BT has successfully ensured that its customers interact in a way that ensures that many tell their friends about the site and its features (competitions, previews, downloads etc.) and return (and may keep paying online phone charges at the same time!).

5 Convenience and ease – the need to make things easier for current and potential customers

This remains one of the most popular and easily understood benefits: the ability to get anything you want from anywhere in the world, at any time. Now that this has become clearly established in the minds of customers, a process that took place from the mid-1990s to the end of the twentieth century, the need is to take this benefit to new levels of service. The implications for e-commerce transactions are as follows:

- Things need to be *easier* – more effective and convenient. Things need to be easier to find, easier to review and assess, easier to buy. This is already a major driver of change for retailers ranging from remote antique dealers to multinational supermarket chains.
- Things need to be *quicker* – without the hassle of traditional channels. A classic example of this would be online banking. Why write cheques, complete payment forms and post payments for utilities when your banking can be done swiftly, online – at 3am on a hilltop (or 7pm in your office) if that is what you prefer. Online transactions also need to be clear and easy to complete.
- Things need to be *problem free* – without the delays of queuing, the uncertainty of whether something is in stock or available, and with the time to think and reflect. Buying airline tickets online is one example; preparing the way online for a car purchase is another, where customers consider everything from the accessories they want to the finance package they can afford, all from the comfort of their own home.

Clearly, accomplishing all of these objectives in a web site is an immense challenge, and one that is very much dependent on the specific product or service being sold. However, there are general aspects to achieving these aims. Make sure that the site is simple to use, easy to navigate with clear, unambiguous labels, and logically organised. Search functions need to be intuitive, reflecting likely customer searches, and ordering needs to be clear and easy. The site needs to be visually appealing with graphics that are quick to load, even on a modest modem connection. The site must also be secure and completely stable, with no bugs or dead ends.

It is a common mistake to assume that achieving these aims requires technological solutions and a separate focus on the online aspect of the business. Online activities can only succeed effectively in partnership with other offline activities, such as customer focus in product development and effective customer support. Many customers experience problems ordering online. One of the most common customer complaints (experienced by possibly as many as 10 per cent of all online purchasers) is that they never receive the goods they have ordered, yet they are still billed and have a difficult and time-consuming experience trying to rectify the situation. The consequences of this for the retailer and the brand can be completely devastating. It is therefore worth considering how the customer can be supported if things should go wrong: the mechanisms that are in place to recover the situation, as well as how to prevent problems in the first place. For some industries that have not traditionally focused on customer service, this may actually provide a new source of competitive advantage.

However, it is certainly worth bearing in mind that asking your customers to do more may suit them by providing more direct control, but asking them to do *too much* may negate any benefits of simplicity. This is particularly the case if you are asking customers for information that is of more direct benefit to you, the business (for example, helping with inventory control or database building) than to them, the customer. It is therefore important to assess each issue or feature from customers' viewpoint, ensure that what customers need to do is simple and that the benefits are clear, and if necessary provide a ready and effective source of offline support.

6 Connectivity – the need to connect with other sites and users online

The issue of connectivity essentially falls into two domains: first, the need for users and customers to be connected –

physically as well as in more intangible 'emotional' ways – with your business, meaning your site, value proposition and brand. Second, the need for sites to connect with each other in a way that adds value for the customer and drives traffic for the business.

Connecting with customers

This issue focuses on the need to ensure that the site is both compelling and 'sticky' so that customers want to stay longer and return more often, preferably having told their friends about it. Connecting with customers can be achieved by demonstrating a good understanding of customers and providing a source of useful and unique information or service for them. The keys are to focus on content, providing reasons for the customer to stay, as well as incentives for the customer to return. Content issues were mentioned earlier, and incentives typically include online loyalty programmes and membership schemes.

Connecting with other sites

There are many similarities between online and offline purchasing, but one of the key differences is that while one would rarely show a customer an alternative shop or service in the offline world, there are very definite benefits to doing this in the online world. This belief is frequently a source of contention among web developers and particularly with those businesses migrating from the offline to the online world, possibly for the first time. However, connecting users to other sites is one means of adding value to your own site, as well as reaching a mutually beneficial arrangement that drives traffic for both sites. An example of this might be a sport retailer's web site and a news and weather site. Both benefit from traffic and visitors, both activities can be complementary and visitors to one may be interested in visiting the other, driving traffic. As with the other critical drivers of e-business, the key is to focus on the customer's likely wants and interests.

When connecting with other web sites it is important that the linked sites are relevant, appropriate, varied, of a similar quality and complementary to your approach, product and message. Linking with everyone is counter-productive: you need to link with sites where your customers are, or where they may want to be. The pay-off for your site is increased traffic and added value – and even the chance of basking in the reflective glory of your partner's brand! This highlights the important notion that connecting with other sites is *reciprocal*, meaning that other sites will similarly benefit from connecting with your business. This may have a number of advantages, but foremost among these is the financial benefit. The potential for generating revenue or using links to reduce costs as part of a barter exchange with a supplier or partner, for example, can be significant.

7 Cost and profitability – the need to reduce waste, improve financial efficiency and drive profits

It amazes me how often otherwise sane and successful business people can rush into developing a web site, completely oblivious to the need to ensure that the site is profitable. Occasionally this can be masked by the view that 'if we build it they will come', or it's a loss leader, or we need it to keep in step with our competitors. I have seen all of these excuses used across a variety of industries (frankly, by people who should know better!) to justify massive investments in online activities. The truth is that investing in a successful web site is *always* expensive, and the strategy – the objectives, priorities and benefits – needs to be clearly understood and planned in the same way as any other major business investment.

The financial benefits of web sites are often over-shadowed by a focus on customers, and while this is certainly a fundamentally important benefit (after all, without customers what else is there?), there are still important gains to be had by focusing on financial issues of cost control and profit maximisation. To ensure the financial success of the web site it is important to do the following:

- *Complete a profitability projection for the site that matches the business objectives.* The development of the site needs to be underpinned by a financial plan: how much will it cost? What is the likely return and over what period? What are the key performance indicators for the site? What are the main financial priorities for the site? These might be increasing prices, increasing average revenue per client, reducing the average cost per transaction, improving payment times, improving the efficiency of marketing campaigns, enhancing the appeal, profile and hence value of the brand, or any one of a number of other financial measures. The financial performance of the site then needs to be measured against the chosen priorities, with action taken if expectations are not met.

- *Secure and plan the necessary level of investment.* It is a mistake to believe that online developments are going to be cheap, and it is equally a mistake to believe that costs will be static or fail to rise. Investment plans need to acknowledge the need for enhancement and possibly also technological development. As well as planning for the initial development and subsequent upgrade of the site, running costs need to be understood and secured.

- *Use the site to eliminate waste, ensuring lean operations and cost reductions.* While web sites are not cheap to establish, they can provide an invaluable means of reducing on-going trading and transaction costs. It is important when developing the site to consider how it can increase efficiency and reduce waste. For example, an FAQ section or online access for customers to their account may reduce the number of staff needed in call centres to handle customer queries. Enabling customers to order directly via the business's order-processing system can ensure that order handling is streamlined, providing a quicker and more efficient process for the customer and a cheaper one for the business. The need for extensive inventories and work-in-progress can also be reduced by linking customer orders with suppliers, helping to deliver products just in time (rather than just too late).

- *Use the Internet for supplier management, value chain analysis and outsourcing.* It tends to be assumed that web-enabled e-commerce relates to mass-market products and services, whereas some of the most valuable and far-reaching achievements of e-commerce have been made in the area of business-to-business trade. Complex and high-value businesses like the automotive industry and IT hardware have been among the first to use intranets to manage their work flows, sharing and using information to deliver lean production, efficiency and improvements in cost and timeliness. An efficient, Internet-enabled business can also find it much easier to outsource those aspects of its activities that are not its core area of business or expertise, again by sharing information instantly with its business partners for the benefit of the customer.

- *Provide financial advantages for the customer trading online, passing on some of the benefits and savings and further increasing profits.* It is fitting to come back to the customer directly and consider how they might benefit financially from e-commerce. This might include the possibility of combining finance with other innovations, providing a potential source of competitive advantage. The Web frequently enables customers to sample a product, or receive part of a product for free, or benefit from repeat or online purchasing. In addition, the customer may be willing to pay higher prices for an enhanced online service. (Pricing is a key element of e-commerce and this is explored later in the book.)

8 Customisation – the need to deliver efficient personalisation

The increasing importance of the Internet for supplying adaptive products and services – products that are efficiently personalised for the customer – is evident from developments across a range of industries. The need to match what the individual customer wants with what the product actu-

> **KEY CONCEPT**
>
> Supplying a customised product requires a business to interact with customers to develop that product continuously. The product has to be constantly remade to reflect changes as both the customer and the company 'learn', and probably the only way that this can be accomplished cost-effectively is via the Internet.

ally delivers is the key to success and competitive advantage. For example, information publishers that break down the material they publish into a dynamically evolving electronic library of information – searchable, accessible, sold and delivered online – can derive a major new source of revenue at relatively little extra cost. This approach can also address the challenges of evolving market forces (where information is already available for free) and dynamically meet customers' needs at the same time. Another example is Peapod.com, a leading US-based online grocery store that has developed personalised sites for its thousands of members; these include a list of individual favourites together with itemised details of the last five orders that each customer placed. Clearly, this is merging customisation with connectivity, convenience and ease and customer care for mutual benefit.

The concept of mass customisation or efficient person-alisation is surprisingly difficult to master. Several factors are critical to success, including:

- *The need to plan this development from the outset* rather than simply trying to graft it on to the web site later.
- *Ensuring that products can be configured to meet each individual customer's requirements* through a process of dialogue and probing.
- *Ensuring that customers are aware of exactly what they can choose, and what they cannot.* For example, an online retailer can provide you with details, as often as you like, of products (books, music etc.) that meet a specific taste, but they may only be able to offer three types of delivery service: 'standard' (5-day delivery), 'urgent' (48-hour delivery) and 'stop the world now, I must have it' (perhaps 12-hour delivery).
- *Constantly developing and refining the service so that it meets customers' needs and stays ahead of competitors.* Services are good examples of this approach, where a financial services company might develop new products (e.g. insurance policies or investment plans) that meet the specific and different requirements of each individual customer. This requires suppliers to be prepared to deliver this service, and internal processes clearly also need to be configured to provide it.

9 Capability – the need to ensure that your site remains dynamic, responsive and flexible

The issue of customisation highlights the need for capability: being able to act dynamically and use your web site as a business driver, not a static monolith that was massively impressive once but is now looking like a dinosaur. Equally dangerous is the 'dinosaur strain', when your web site has dinosaur potential because it is simply not prepared to change and adapt. This issue links closely with the need to focus on organisational culture, encouraging people to perceive the Internet as a dynamic tool for meeting customer needs. It also relates to how well the site is managed: what objectives are set, how they are implemented and how they are measured and monitored.

Case Study: General Electric and the power of extranets to increase capability[3]

In 1996 the General Electric company, one of America's most successful businesses of the last twenty years, if not the last century, pioneered the use of an extranet (a closed network for use by people external to the organisation) in its lighting division to develop effective business-to-business relationships. GE's lighting division established a network linking with its suppliers worldwide so that it could swiftly complete all of its purchasing transactions. A feature of the extranet, known as the Trade Processing Network (TPN), was the facility allowing GE's many varied international suppliers to download GE product specifications and communicate with the company via a secure, encrypted software link over the Internet.

The benefits of this approach for the lighting division were swift and significant: the cycle time in the purchasing process was reduced, enabling much more efficient working and inventory management. GE suppliers became an integrated part of a global community. Furthermore, TPN was employed in seven other GE business divisions as well as being licensed to other manufacturers to use with their suppliers.

One bold approach is to involve your customers in your business via your web site by asking what they want, and then acting on that information, or by asking what they think of your ideas and plans. Capability is often best delivered by a development process and mindset that allow product testing. This is also supported by the dynamic and creative ethos of the Internet. Test an idea: if it works then repeat, develop or extend it; if it nearly works then refine it; if it fails then consider why, before backing out of that blind alley and trying again.

10 Competitiveness – the need to be distinctive

The success of any strategy is relative. A strategy may be well conceived and executed, it may even succeed in achieving its aims, but if it is outmanoeuvred by its competitors the result is usually failure; this is certainly the case with e-business developments that are, by their nature, prone to rapid and dramatic change. Therefore there is a need to focus on the success of the strategy *relative* to other market developments. The requirement to be competitive underpins all of the other critical drivers of e-business success. Figure 2.2 highlights the sources of competition for e-businesses. It is interesting to note that internal competition from within the same organisation – so-called *cannibalising* of markets – is seen as a source of competition by 7 per cent of respondents.

One key finding from this Internet survey is that however amazing the pace and scope of online change may be, it is still the traditional competitor that matters most. This may be small businesses that are expanding, or large businesses that are opening up new fronts to develop their profits and market share. It is certainly the case that in recent years a dispro-portionate amount of publicity has been given to the 'dot-com' revolution; the Internet is a powerful new area of

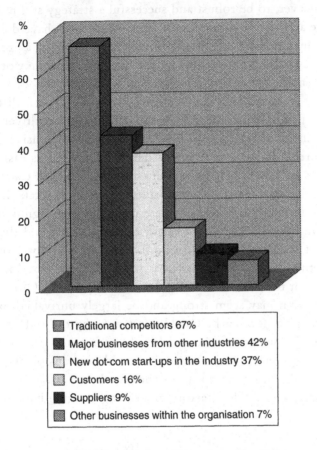

Traditional competitors 67%
Major businesses from other industries 42%
New dot-com start-ups in the industry 37%
Customers 16%
Suppliers 9%
Other businesses within the organisation 7%

Figure 2.2: Perceived sources of competition in the new economy

Source: Aggregation of information from the EIU and other online information sources[2] (January 2001)

competition, but many of the competitors are existing 'old-economy' businesses struggling to establish themselves and find the best approach. While there are some high-profile successes, I believe that there are actually many more businesses whose online activities are mediocre at best.

However, to be robust and successful a strategy still needs to take account of competition: what competitors have done, are doing and may do in the future. When developing a profit-driven e-business, it can also be useful to consider the worst-case scenario: what would happen if . . . In this way, an Internet strategy can often be made more durable and realistic.

The factors with the greatest influence on competitiveness online include *organisational issues*, such as how the business is structured. This may encompass factors as diverse as cash reserves and supply chains and distribution channels. *Cultural issues*, encompassing how the business views its markets, how flexible it is and how decisions are made, are also significant. *Resource issues* such as the strength of the business and the Internet trends that are affecting it also have an impact on competitiveness, strengthening or weakening the e-business in relation to its current and potential competitors. Often an organisation may seem strong and be largely unrivalled, but this complacency can be quickly destroyed by the sudden arrival of new, innovative and largely unexpected (or worse, dismissed) competitors. *Market issues* and how customers perceive the organisation, in essence the brand values that it possesses, are also key factors influencing competitiveness online.

Developing sources of competitive advantage

It is important that online businesses develop a keen sense of market awareness, keeping up-to-date information about their competitors and, in particular, how these businesses are perceived in the market. Maintaining awareness across a range of issues will help to identify where online competitors are strong, and where they are weak and open to competition. It can also help in analysing sources of competitive advantage. Key issues to consider about competitors (whether competing online or not) include understanding the following aspects of competitors:

- pricing policies and the value proposition as a whole;
- customers' perceptions of your business, your main competitors and market developments in general;
- brand reputation and recognition – who is the market leader and why?
- other external perceptions, including the views of bankers, journalists, financial markets (where relevant) and suppliers;
- product quality;
- service levels;
- product portfolio;
- business structure and organisation, notably their size, whether they enjoy economies of scale, the type of employees they attract, the amount they spend on training, their expenditure on product development, their distribution channels;
- the timing of promotional campaigns, whether they offer special promotions, and the main sales channels used;
- flexibility and organisational culture;
- staff loyalty;
- customer loyalty;
- financial structure and cash reserves.

Using the ten drivers to benefit your e-business

There are two additions to these ten factors that are also vital to success: *continuity* and *commitment*. It is too often the case that businesses regard these developments as transient or requiring an initial push and little else. Each of the ten drivers needs its own plan or approach to achieve success, and it is also important to understand that they all change dynamically. It is necessary, therefore, to ensure that they are continuously improved and that there is sufficient commitment to each one.

All of these factors, which have long been common to achieving competitiveness, are encompassed in the ten critical drivers of e-business success. When planning the development of your e-business activities, it can be useful to assess the relevance of each of these factors to your customers, your brand, your product offer and your overall business strategy and direction. The advantage of this approach is that at the core of each of these ten factors is the need for a clear focus on the target customer.

Leading and building the online business

CHAPTER 3

Overview

Setting direction is only the start: success requires a range of different leadership styles and approaches, from democratic and consensual to authoritative and autocratic, depending on the range of online initiatives and opportunities and their stage of development. Leading, attracting, retaining and empowering people are key drivers of success online. However, in the fast-evolving, flat hierarchies that characterise most modern organisations, leadership is all too often about simply 'hanging on'. Competitive advantage and greater profitability therefore come to the business that can proactively *drive* success, demonstrating genuine flexibility and harnessing innovation and enterprise. The skills and sensitivity required to lead a profitable online business are outlined in this chapter, providing leaders with the best approach and tools for their specific situation and challenges.

This chapter recognises that e-business is changing the nature of work – not only in the obvious ways but also in subtle, intangible ways, that have a direct impact

CONTINUED ... **Overview**

on leadership issues such as loyalty, motivation, innovation and empowerment. The opportunities need to be dynamically exploited and this chapter will:

- Highlight practical techniques for leading a business through the process of change resulting from the impact of the Internet. This also includes highlighting the dangers that can arise (e.g. lack of control, co-ordination, communication, poor decision making, low morale and staff turnover) and how these can be prevented or resolved.
- Help senior managers to design and develop a structure (or architecture) for the business that is competitive, flexible and appropriate.
- Provide a guide to the key issues that should be considered when developing an online strategy.

Leading the business through change

A wide range of complex and inter-related factors, such as the market, people, product, environment and industry, determines the business culture of any organisation. The culture of the business in turn affects how receptive the organisation or business unit is to change, and how that change needs to be implemented. It is important to be completely clear from the start about the need for leadership to embrace change thoroughly. Leading a profit-driven business of any size requires dynamism, flexibility and the ability to embrace change. It is precisely this requirement that has driven the explosion in size, prominence and value of the Internet. However, the Internet is also one of the greatest ever *enablers* of business. The situation is therefore one of symbiosis, with organisations driving the development of the Internet, and online trends driving the development (or at the very least affecting the success) of almost every business. Business leadership is about achieving success during a time of rapid and constant change; change, in turn, is very largely about e-commerce.[4]

Creating and delivering major change

Few subjects are as important, frequently discussed or misunderstood as leadership. It is central to the success of organisations, yet leadership can be hardest to deliver during times of change and uncertainty: it is hard both to lead and to be led. However, with an increasing rate of change being one of the few constants in the modern workplace and one of the furthest-reaching effects of the development of business online, leadership is a skill that must be mastered to ensure profitability online.

Change is apparent in a wide variety of situations: everything from major issues such as restructuring, mergers or downsizing, to more routine measures such as introducing new business models, products, systems and resources. Fortunately, there are *processes* that can enable leaders to deliver major change and *skills* that will help to implement change and achieve progress and these are detailed below.

1 Ensure that senior managers understand the key issues and potential impact of the online environment on their business

Many senior managers are wary and sceptical of the Internet – usually with good reason! There are many examples of hype, bad management practice, poor strategies and, above all, incessant risk inherent in the shifting nature of e-commerce. It can help to view e-commerce developments not as a separate area of operation, but as a business tool supporting and driving all aspects of an organisation's activities. To take an example, nobody talked of 'telephone business' during the first part of the twentieth century: telephony simply became an integrated, everyday part of business with many

> **KEY CONCEPT**
>
> Education, explanation and continuous development of ideas and issues are frequently overlooked components of success for online businesses. The need for senior managers to facilitate and engage in this process is vital.

commercial applications. So it is with e-commerce and online developments, and understanding the scope of its impact and integration with business activities are therefore vital.

If senior managers do not feel comfortable with the application of online technology, or if they dismiss it, this can lead inexorably to avoidance, cynicism and delay. This, in turn, leaves the business highly vulnerable to attack from online competitors. The key to breaking or preventing this cycle is therefore to educate senior managers, ensuring that they understand where the financial, brand and market risks lie; what the impact of online developments might be; and where the potential benefits could arise (and how they might be achieved).

2 Establish a sense of urgency

The next step is to establish and communicate a sense of urgency. This helps in a number of ways. First, urgency wakes people up to the need to act, to focus on the task at hand and to be at their best. All of these are essential if success is to be achieved. Second, it shows the team that there is someone who is both concerned about the situation and in charge. During times of uncertainty, people can behave at their best and their worst, and a sense of urgency helps to establish clear authority. Finally, in practical terms urgency also sets out the priorities: rather than stay paralysed, people are given focus and direction about what needs to be done, as well as their role in the process.

At this stage, all leaders need to start by identifying and discussing crises, potential crises or major opportunities that could arise. Discussing these issues with others, in particular with those being led, will help to communicate urgency, while at the same time giving ownership and helping to solve the problem. For leaders in a highly competitive business or a market with great potential that may be evolving rapidly, there needs to be an assessment of the market and competitive realities. This will identify immediate actions and also help to decide priorities – but most of all, it will reinforce the benefits of urgency.

3 Create a guiding coalition to lead change in the e-business

One of the features of Internet-driven change is that it spreads: it is invariably hard to contain and it impacts across a wide range of areas – often where and when it is least expected! The business leader should therefore establish a guiding coalition or group with enough power to lead the change, and get that group to work together as a team. To be effective, the guiding coalition must represent all of the areas affected by the change and understand the likely effects. It should therefore include people representing customers and finance, as well as product development and technology. The coalition must have sufficient resources (particularly market information) to ensure that it has all the facts and can take the necessary action. However, perhaps even more important than possessing adequate resources is having the authority to lead the change, acting decisively and sensitively in every-thing from setting the strategy and executing action to monitoring the process.

In creating a group to guide the development of new business initiatives, it is also important to gain the confidence of the people being led. This can be achieved by displaying sufficient confidence in other members of the coalition, while at the same time, when appropriate, testing and reassuring colleagues about the approach being taken. Possessing the 'soft' skills needed to communicate and motivate people during a time of uncertainty is clearly an asset here and these skills need to be part of the team.

4 Develop a vision and strategy for your online activities

From the outset, the leader and the guiding coalition must create a vision to direct the change effort. This needs to include clear goals and timescales. They then need to start carefully developing strategies for achieving that vision (the priorities for achieving this were explored in detail in Chapter 2). It is worth considering that while leaders must develop a clear vision for how the online business will work, the *pursuit* and *implementation* of that vision can often be experimental. This is highlighted in point 7 below: the need to generate short-term wins and gain momentum. The idea is to develop a hypothesis and think through key issues in advance, and then establish the best possible presence online as quickly as possible. Once that is up and running, it is desirable to use the Internet to collect feedback so that the site and overall value proposition can be modified, responding effectively to changing market requirements. The key is therefore to get established quickly and possibly on a small scale at first (if necessary, without being seduced by grand designs or massive investment plans) and then aggressively to follow through with on-going modifications based on market feedback.

5 Communicate the change vision

Communication is fundamental to success – without it, no amount of research and planning will work. Employees need to know what is happening, what their role is, how they are progressing and where the limits to their authority lie. Communication is therefore much more than simply telling people what to do and trying to encourage them. In particular, the leader should use every means possible to communicate the new vision and ensure that the guiding coalition provides a role model for employees' behaviour.

6 Empower broad-based action at all levels (as a response to constantly evolving market conditions)

Empowering people is important at any time, but for the business concerned with developing its online activities it is critical for success. Change frequently requires quick, decisive action based on evolving circumstances and closeness to the action. Often, this action is best taken by people who understand the strategy and goals and who are empowered – they have the authority and confidence to act. To empower people, leaders need to remove obstacles and difficulties, including lack of training and confidence in technological issues. Also important is the need to change systems or structures that undermine the vision for change; these can often be traditional methods of working that were relevant to a different set of market conditions, probably even pre-dating the commercial exploitation and development of the Internet. Finally, the empowering e-business leader needs to encourage risk taking, innovation and non-traditional ideas.

7 Generate short-term wins and create momentum

The business leader needs to provide clear momentum for the process of change. The nature of change in the online world means that it is self-sustaining, with one change leading to another, cascading through the organisation. However, if one part changes but the process halts, the organisation can be severely handicapped and left in a dysfunctional state. Confusion reigns: what is the best approach, how flexible should the organisation be, should the process continue (if so, in what direction) or should the business try to retreat to the position it started from? This confusion is avoided if the process has momentum and confidence, and to achieve this the leader must plan for visible improvements in performance, or 'wins', and work hard to create those wins. It is also important to visibly recognise and reward people who made the wins possible. This both motivates and leads by example.

8 Consolidate gains and produce more change

The next step is for the leader to use the increasing momentum to change all of the systems, structures and policies that don't fit together and don't fit the transformation vision. This can include, for example, hiring, promoting and developing people who can implement the change vision, as well as reinvigorating the process with new projects, themes and change agents. Clearly there is a cost to this, but there can be a greater cost in doing too little or acting too late. Once the change process is started momentum needs to be sustained, as the alternative can often be just as costly.

9 Anchor new approaches in the organisational culture

The final stage is one of the most important and, if not completed properly, can undermine all that has been achieved. The new ways of working, systems and approach need to be sustained and embedded in the organisation. A new approach will be required for a constantly evolving set of circumstances and to continue educating people about what needs to be done. For the leader this means creating better performance through both customer- and productivity-oriented behaviour and through more and better leadership. It also requires the leader to articulate the connections between new behaviours and organisational success, as well as developing the means to ensure leadership development and succession.

Anchoring new attitudes and approaches to e-commerce can be achieved by establishing the right architecture for your business (including online) activities, which is discussed later in this chapter.

Vital questions and answers

. . . for leaders wanting to empower people to effect change

1 Have you communicated a clear, powerful vision to your team (or employees)?

If people have a shared sense of purpose, it will be easier to initiate actions to achieve that purpose. Many visions for online businesses focus, quite sensibly, on markets and customers above all.

2 Have you created conditions and an environment compatible with the vision?

Structures need to be in place that support action; structures that are out of step block necessary action. The culture of the organisation also needs to be correct and appropriate to the dynamic, flexible online environment, with emphasis on values such as being blame free, open and honest.

3 Have you provided the training that employees need?

Without the right skills and attitudes people feel disempowered, lacking in confidence and not achieving their potential. This is particularly the case with new technological developments.

4 Are information and personnel systems aligned to the vision?

If systems are out of step they will also block necessary flexibility, responsiveness and action. It is little use building a dynamic, talented team to drive your online

CONTINUED ... **Vital questions and answers**

activities and profits, only to bury them under a mountain of inappropriate bureaucracy.

5 Are you prepared to confront supervisors who undercut necessary change?

Remember that nothing disempowers people the way a bad manager can, and often the online environment leaves many people feeling uncertain and even concerned. This needs to be addressed and managed, or else fear, trepidation and uncertainty can combine to form cynicism and a resistance to change.

6 Do you, as a leader, focus yourself and others on the questions that every person – at every level in the organisation – needs to ask continuously?

- *Purpose* – What am I (what are we) trying to do? It is vital to know what needs to be done and where the priorities lie for your online activities.
- *Winning* – How do we gain and sustain a competitive advantage?
- *Timeliness* – What is the best use of my time, right now?
- *Change* – How do we recognise the need for change and how will we bring it about when needed?
- *Action* – How do we deliver the desired results?

To answer these questions it is necessary to keep constantly in touch with the development of the business: the process of change can be eroded both by remoteness and by the *perception* of remoteness. In addition, communicating, listening and persuading, as well as

CONTINUED . . . Vital questions and answers

telling, are extremely valuable. Finally, testing your
own assumptions, asking for advice or admitting to
yourself when you need additional help are necessary
elements of the business leader's approach to online
activities.

7   Are you aware of some of the pitfalls of leading an
Internet-driven change process?

There are three main danger areas for a business leader,
and they don't only apply to online developments. First,
be sensitive: change at any time is difficult. Constant
technological change is particularly exciting, but also
daunting and demanding for most people. Second, *work
smart and avoid acting too quickly*: it is important with any
major decision to ensure that you have all the facts and
have considered all options. Finally, *don't forget to follow
through*. You need to make sure that change is anchored in
the organisation and accepted. Don't finish too early and,
while the battle may be won, remember that the war
carries on!

Designing the best structure for online business success

Developing the best e-commerce structure

The term 'e-commerce structure' is not intended to imply a
static, monolithic approach; rather, it refers to both the
business process and the enabling technology needed to
implement the business vision online. As with the business

vision and strategy, the e-commerce structure is entirely about *competitiveness*, implementing a dynamic strategy through a changing, dynamic medium. To be really effective, the e-commerce architecture usually needs to address the following organisational and commercial issues.

One of the first stages is to consider partnering with an Internet service provider (ISP). The business has to design its e-commerce value proposition and then deliver on the commercial potential by, for example, driving traffic to the site, but the risk of building and maintaining the technology that runs the site is outsourced to the ISP. In this way, if the e-commerce application fails the risk is reduced (usually, companies will simply pay a monthly fee to the ISP and not have too onerous a notice period for termination).

Whether or not an ISP is selected, there are several elements to consider, including site design, product offer, sales process (and tools such as online shopping carts), payment terms, security, delivery and distribution, taxes, customer tracking and data mining, special-offer promotions and customer loyalty. The first stage is planning and establishing the site. Design of the site or online store is an important starting point. While there are general rules for web site design intended to ensure that the site is *sticky* (meaning that customers stick to it while they are there, as well as returning to it later), what matters most is that the site *works best for the customer*. Understanding the target customer is therefore vital to achieving success. This approach also needs to be commensurate with the brand, and if the business's brand values are not associated with the online offering it is certainly worth considering how to extend your business brand into cyberspace.

Building and displaying catalogues, also known as brochureware, are one of the first places organisations start when developing their online activities. The business needs to

be clear about the product offer and emphasise the benefits.
The catalogue also needs to use the online medium,
informing and exciting the customer in an immediate way and
having the flexibility to be updated with amendments relating
to new products, special offers and price changes.

Case Study: The EIU online store

One of the most inventive Internet sites for international
businesses is the online store developed by the
Economist Intelligence Unit (eiu.com). The store
effectively takes the EIU's offline brand identity and
reputation for informed, international analysis of
political, economic and commercial issues for senior
executives, and uses its core strengths to attract and
retain existing and new customers. This approach is in
preference to simply transplanting this on to a web site (a
failing of many traditional publishers). The critical
drivers of e-commerce success are used so that, for
example, visitors can raise queries, communicate and
connect. However, above all the EIU leverages its core
content expertise so that not only is the design of the site
sticky and compelling, but it also displays innovative
new features and business information.

By using its existing strengths and strategic resources,
including people, customers and brand, the EIU has
determinedly made the ambitious and risky move from
the traditional offline environment to the online one,
while also enhancing profitability.

Moving on from the planning stage means building an
e-commerce structure that facilitates customer transactions
online. Shopping carts are one popular way for customers to
buy, but this has significant implications for credit card

payments and security. To accept credit card payments via the Internet, businesses need a merchant account with the card provider, as well as encryption technology to make online shopping secure (another advantage of using an ISP). All aspects of the order process need to be assessed and piloted from the customer's viewpoint, and this process will highlight, for example, the fact that once an order has been placed the web site's sales system must calculate the costs of shipping and taxes.

Continuously adding value to the site is another important area of consideration, and this is best achieved by data mining – tracking and capturing data about each individual customer and purchase. This information can be used in an aggregated form to enhance the site generally, as well as using specific customer data to add value to the relationship with each individual customer. Finally, merchandising and promoting items of special interest for clearly defined customer groups forms another method of adding value.

Techniques for establishing the best structure for your e-commerce activities

Assess your position: the five stages of e-commerce development

It is worth considering what can be called the five stages of e-commerce development (Figure 3.1) and assessing your organisation's development along this process. This will help you to assess where you need to consolidate, where you are starting anew, and how this can best be executed. It is important to emphasise that although it is possible for businesses to jump from stage to stage – indeed, this may be essential in order to compete – each stage feeds into the next one and is sequential. This means, for example, that once one

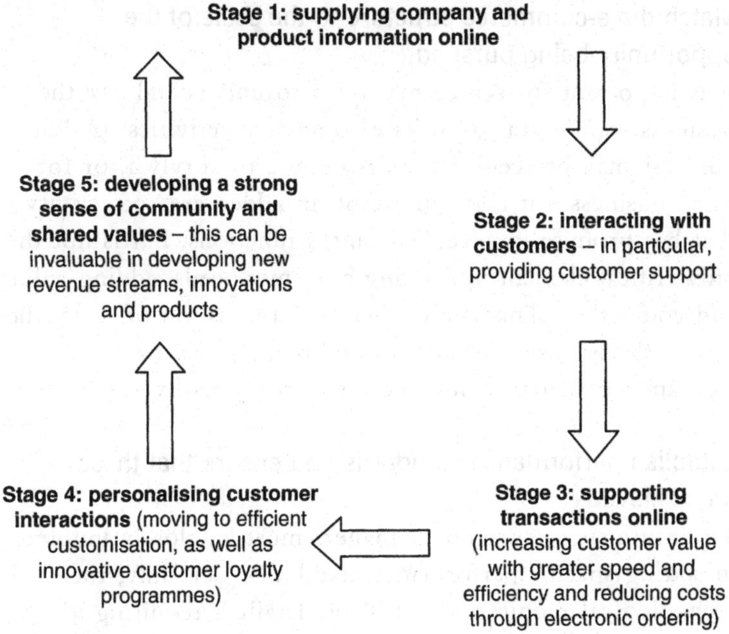

Stage 1: supplying company and product information online

Stage 5: developing a strong sense of community and shared values – this can be invaluable in developing new revenue streams, innovations and products

Stage 2: interacting with customers – in particular, providing customer support

Stage 4: personalising customer interactions (moving to efficient customisation, as well as innovative customer loyalty programmes)

Stage 3: supporting transactions online (increasing customer value with greater speed and efficiency and reducing costs through electronic ordering)

Figure 3.1: The five stages of e-commerce development

cycle has been completed, the level of success achieved at stage 5 can be fed back into the online company and product information that is supplied.[5]

Establish the vision and build the team

Clearly, the business's e-commerce structure needs to result from the organisation's strategy. To be successful, this approach relies on the strategy having been developed from a clear understanding of customer needs – along with the market opportunities and the competitive action required to meet those needs. Once the vision is agreed, it needs to be cascaded through the business and effectively implemented. The key to achieving this is building a team that has both the skills and resources to carry out the vision.

Match the e-commerce structure to the scale of the opportunity being pursued

It is important for senior managers to understand *how* the business should approach its e-commerce activities. Online business may be seen as the only route to survival, or for some businesses it may simply be an added area of activity that has promise in several business functions, but is not the only critical element in meeting customer needs, adding value and competing. This comes down to a question of scale: the size of the opportunity needs to be reflected in the size of the e-commerce structure and the resources it receives.

Establish performance standards and ensure that these are achieved

To ensure success, senior managers must be closely involved in setting specific performance standards. Certainly, the technological requirements will be detailed, requiring valuable specialist skills, and will vary between businesses; the senior manager's input here may well be limited. Of much greater importance is the need to set challenging and ambitious targets for return on investment, security, market share, level of online business, repeat business and average revenue per customer, as well as internal issues such as time to market, speed of response, cost reductions and other business measures. Guiding all of these targets is the need to add value for the customer in a competitive way. It can help when setting performance measures for these to be tightly defined and carefully quantified, with clear deadlines and milestones for their effective implementation.

However, establishing performance measures that are competitive, realistic and challenging for the business is only the start: senior managers need to work at this issue on an on-going basis. This requires managers to keep in close contact with market developments, customer expectations, techno-logical developments (which may enable greater levels of service and value for the customer) and competition. Putting in place processes to ensure that this can be achieved is vital, and the performance standards and business structure clearly need to adapt and evolve, in order to take account of market developments.

Adapt swiftly and effectively to change

Change is the driver of growth and opportunity on the Internet, but it is also a source of threat and instability, particularly if the business structure is not flexible or able to adapt easily. The e-commerce structure needs to be able to effect change in two ways: reactively and proactively. On the reactive side is the need to be able to react to systemic problems when these arise. Problems can vary widely, including issues as diverse as network interruptions and departures of key staff. A business risk analysis is a useful tool for senior managers, as it can help to prepare for interruptions and difficulties. Ultimately, however, business leaders need to understand the need for investment in online activities, and this may mean adding more capacity, further insurance and expensive technology to ensure that customers are not adversely affected by system interruptions. If problems do arise and they are not resolved swiftly and to the customers' benefit, the consequences for customer loyalty, the brand and the long-term success of the business can be disastrous.

The second area of change is also inevitable in the online environment driven by technology: the need for the business structure to be able to anticipate (and preferably drive or manipulate) fluctuations in demand. Demand growth is one of the most overlooked elements of online trading. Businesses either build vast behemoths that are too expensive and too soon for the market, or else they build inadequate sites and back-office processes that creak and collapse under the weight of demand, often resulting in that demand disappearing, never to return. Organisations need to monitor market developments, designing their e-commerce teams and structures so that they have the resources and ability required to keep ahead of market developments and changes in demand.

Online strategy

Drivers of online strategy developments

Organising a business so that it can succeed online is a daunting task: the scale of the costs, operations, risk – and simply the tasks involved – is significant. However, not all firms that operate online are large, and those that succeed understand the reasons for developing their activities online and respond accordingly. For the established business the drivers of online developments include:

- *Competitive pressures* – either because online competitors are entering core markets, or because the level of competition in markets online is much lower (enabling the business to make a greater profit).
- *Market pressures* because existing markets are saturated, because there are new and developing opportunities for trading using the Internet, or because the market as a whole works best online.
- *Development expertise* or other resources for production (from a receptive customer base to in-house expertise) may be available and need to be harnessed.
- *Economies of scale* – getting the greatest possible value out of the existing business – can be achieved by broadening the scope of activities, becoming web enabled and selling online.

Online strategy is not just about selling but covers a much wider range of other activities, linking closely with issues such as market-entry strategy, acquisition strategy and product development. This section focuses on how to develop a strategy for profitable online operations.

 IMPLEMENTATION CHECKLIST: key issues to review when developing an online strategy

Key issues to consider as part of the development of an online strategy include the following:

1 Define the objectives of the strategy

The first priority is to be clear about what an online strategy can and cannot achieve. There are several key issues to resolve when first considering online operations, including:

- What is the organisation trying to achieve?
- How does the online strategy help to achieve the organisation's overall aims?
- What are the priorities?
- What are the commercial options and parameters (e.g. joint venture, franchising, manufacturing, licensing)?
- Where are the potential pitfalls?
- How will the risk be managed and reduced? (Consider issues such as how much money can be spent, what level of return is expected and when.)
- Does the organisational structure need to be altered to take full advantage of the online operations (and if so, how)?

In answering these questions, it can be helpful to complete a SWOT (strengths, weaknesses, opportunities and threats) analysis for the organisation as a whole, as well as for the new e-commerce operation.

2 Understand the markets that are being entered

As with any entry into a new market or area of operation, it pays to understand how progress is made, how things are done and what the key issues are. These can include assessing and understanding the following:

◆ *Cultural issues* such as how the organisation will be perceived. Is everyone involved prepared for doing business in an environment that may well be different? Cultural issues are less significant than they once were, but it is certainly the case that the rise of the Internet has resulted in organisations being less bureaucratic and generally more dynamic (or at least aware of the need for dynamism and customer responsiveness). One solution is simply to recognise the cultural differences, show flexibility and compromise and work hard at developing a unitary set of values and perspectives. Common systems and integrated objectives can help achieve this.

◆ *People issues* are closely linked to the previous point; for instance, are staff prepared, motivated, trained and equipped to do business on the Internet? Practical realities should not be overlooked, as they are often the greatest source of difficulty and barrier to expansion in the short and medium term. Potential concerns and difficulties should not be overlooked: what are the main concerns for the organisation, and for the local area where the business is entering? How will these be monitored?

◆ *Public relations issues* and whether there are opportunities to raise the profile of the organisation and facilitate its entry into the market.

3 Assess the best method of setting up operations online

Analysing the available options for doing business online will help to decide the best approach, and it will also inform the way the approach is executed. For example, the strategy may be to reduce reliance on traditional markets and sell more online. The next step is to decide how best to do this; a decision will be made depending on the nature of the market and the quality of the options available, and from that the priorities will emerge.

For smaller organisations, executing an online strategy inevitably requires a champion – someone with expertise is useful, but someone with dynamism and commitment is essential. This person will need to be flexible enough to make the new strategy succeed. Another valuable approach is to devise a project plan, not simply for focusing activities when the new operation is being established, but also to prioritise activities and focus work for the first few months of the online operation.

4   Structure the organisation's online operations

Restructuring the new online business is frequently useful. It can be unreasonable and a waste of resources to try to make a new Internet business fit the systems and procedures that already exist. At some stage there are several core management issues that need to be reviewed and taken into account in the online business and these are much better tackled early. They include:

- ◆ *Communications*, ensuring that information and expertise flow freely through the organisation. This is much easier than it was, say, 30 years ago, but it does require planning and investment to provide the most appropriate resources. It is also important that best-practice information is widely disseminated and available for everyone in the organisation.
- ◆ *Leadership*, including motivating people, setting direction and decision making, can tend to be different and challenging. The leadership of the organisation needs to

understand this and consider ways of leading and directing without necessarily being present.

◆ *Autonomy and empowerment* need to be confirmed with clear reporting structures, responsibilities and authority levels. Most organisations benefit from being integrated and cohesive and this needs to be considered in the online business. Co-ordination and control are other issues that need to be planned and worked at. Often, if left to drift, online operations become separate entities virtually at war with the rest of the organisation. Contact, co-ordination and control are valuable solutions.

5 Integrating the global organisation

As well as addressing these and other management issues, larger organisations with multiple operations need to consider how to reduce costs and maximise resources with a single, integrated structure, as well as making full use of the resources and specialist expertise in each separate operation.

Selecting the most effective structure depends on the specific needs and priorities of the organisation, and there is certainly no simple solution that fits every situation. Key issues to consider when deciding the best structure include:

◆ regulatory factors;
◆ resource issues, varying in importance from the availability of skilled staff and leaders who can develop the business, to opportunities for raising local finance;
◆ the purpose, size and complexity of the operation: generally, the more sophisticated and complex, the greater the level of autonomy.

6 Communicate

When building an online business it is important that stakeholders in the organisation (notably existing employees, shareholders and financial backers, customers and suppliers) understand what is happening, what the advantages are and what it means for them. Without this explanation rumours and concerns can arise, and organisations can leave themselves open to charges of being distracted or delaying in non-core activities.

7 Consider the financial implications of online business (and remember that, despite projections to the contrary, web sites *always* cost money!)

The financial aspects of global strategy are particularly significant. These include the standard commercial issues of risk, investment and management control of finance associated with any major new undertaking.

Developing an e-commerce or online business can enhance every aspect of the organisation, for example exposing people to new ideas and approaches as well as gaining the commercial advantages of diversity. The risks can be great, but the benefits can also be massive, broadening perspectives and transforming organisations into competitive, inter-national operators. The key issues for achieving success are:

- defining the overall strategy and developing objectives;
- planning the development of the online business so that its success can be sustained;
- understanding what is involved, what can be achieved and where the pitfalls lie;
- managing costs and risk;
- restructuring systems (such as communications and information management) to ensure that the organisation is fully integrated.

Developing your markets to increase profitability

CHAPTER 4

Overview

Understanding markets, the changes wrought by the Internet and how web-based tools can actually *develop* profitability is a key strategic issue – and a major benefit of the Internet. Key issues and techniques to explain are:

- Segmenting markets on the Internet and the fundamental importance of data mining.
- Market drivers and key agents of change, in particular techniques for assessing the impact of the *convergence* of products, businesses, markets and customers. This also involves understanding where an industry and business are heading, how market opportunities appear and how they can be exploited. Many businesses are facing new market structures and expectations, which need to be assessed and turned to the business's advantage, with a permanent but adaptive structure in place to manage on-going changes.

Segmenting markets and data mining

Market segmentation on the Internet

Market segmentation is the process of profiling the target market for a product, so that the business can understand, in as great a level of detail as possible, how best to sell and deliver customer service. Some of the benefits of segmentation include helping to determine customer needs accurately to improve product development, so that products are made more popular by adding features that will increase competitiveness. A second benefit of segmentation is the ability to understand customers and their buying habits, so that marketing plans are relevant, targeted, well implemented and increasingly effective. Finally, segmentation can influence pricing strategies, as it leads to a more detailed understanding of customers and markets.

In the offline world, segmentation involves breaking information down into sections that are highly relevant to the target market and then closely analysing that information. Applying different criteria (such as income, location and age of consumers) to a market can generate tightly focused information, improving the overall effectiveness of product development and marketing.

On the Internet, traditional approaches to market segmentation can be taken to a whole new level of accuracy and value. As the Internet provides access to markets that are global, diverse and complex, market segmentation has become increasingly valuable in maintaining the effectiveness of marketing strategies.

Benefits of segmenting online markets

The benefits of segmentation using the Internet are as follows:

- *Focus.* The value of market segmentation is in highlighting differences and specific characteristics, which requires clarity and focus. The Internet is frequently regarded as a mass medium, but it is also much more a one-to-one medium, particularly when meeting customer needs.

- *Simplicity.* To be effective, market segmentation needs to be clear, rational and simple. Specific products, offers and benefits need to be clearly communicated to each individual customer. This can be achieved using specific customer details acquired through the Internet.

- *Certainty.* It is tempting to jump to conclusions or make assumptions about segments based on past experience. However, these can often be mistaken and a key element in successful segmentation is analysis: not only understanding *how* something is but *why* it is that way, with hard evidence and facts to support these views. Clickstream data from the Internet provides factual evidence of what is happening, almost enabling the vendor to see where their customer's eyeballs are roaming on the web page! This sort of information is vitally important in improving all aspects of the business, from the layout of the site to the offers being displayed.

> **KEY CONCEPT**
>
> It is worth considering that as a communications medium in one vital respect the Internet is much more like radio than television. Although it has global reach, the Internet also has the one-to-one *intimacy* of radio as well as the mass appeal of broadcast TV, and this benefit of intimacy is vitally important when communicating with customers. (However, the importance of the Internet as a visual medium is also vitally important.)

The Internet is a valuable tool for segmenting markets as it enables the profit-driven e-business to:

- understand the organisation and composition of the market;
- target potential customers;
- build the loyalty of existing customers, whether they are migrating from the offline environment or begin as online customers;

- analyse market information and develop the effectiveness of marketing plans.

Types of segmentation

Markets can be segmented into any group, the most appropriate division often depending on factors such as the size and nature of the market and product, as well as the purpose of segmenting the market. Segmentation is used for both consumer and commercial markets and the following categories are frequently used.

- *Commercial markets* – geographic location; type of organisation; job title; size of organisation; customer data. Categories in commercial markets are commonly divided into Standard Industry Classification (SIC) codes for ease of use. For example, customers may be given a range of standard classification codes (e.g. relating to their job title, industry sector, location, company turnover). This is used to allow specialised targeting of sub-groups (e.g. all project managers in the oil industry in Scotland, with a company turnover of more than £10 million).
- *Consumer markets* – geographic location; lifestyle and social groupings; product benefits. (Product benefits are one of the most highly effective methods of segmenting the market on the Internet, as they focus on the key benefits of the product to determine the group that will value them. In achieving this, the concept of psychographic profiles is valuable and increasingly popular, using customer's psychological and demographic features, rather than social status.) Others segmentation methods include occupation (a better method of segmenting markets than social groupings because it is based less on assumption, and is clearly targeted), income, nationality and age.

Case Study: ShopSmart.com – the business that zigged while other dot-coms were zagging

ShopSmart.com is an award-winning e-business that provides a shopping portal where consumers can compare prices on a wide range of products. In a surprisingly short period, its achievements have included becoming the UK's leading shopping portal, with over three million page views in August 2000; becoming one of the UK's leading online retailers together with Jungle, Amazon. co.uk, Amazon.com and Streets Online, and being the first dot-com to offer price comparisons in the UK. ShopSmart.com achieved this by focusing its marketing and market development activities on a continuous yet relatively inexpensive and cost-effective campaign. Some of the factors behind its success are described below:

- A focus on three core business objectives: to become part of the consumer's everyday life, to develop a perception of reliability so that customers feel that the business is established and have any concerns about online shopping allayed by the brand, and to communicate the fact that it is about shopping. (This last point may seem trite, yet it is one of the most commonly quoted concerns about many online businesses that have encountered problems, such as Boo.com and Clickmango.com. Unlike these, ShopSmart does exactly what it says.)
- The effective, practical translation of these objectives into a marketing plan with two prongs: awareness building and communicating the benefits of shopping with ShopSmart. The adoption of a shopping bag as its logo highlights an approach favouring the realistic

CONTINUED . . . Case Study: ShopSmart.com – the business that zigged while other dot-coms were zagging

and practical, rather than falling into the technological and over-designed images adopted by many less successful dot-coms. Other features of the marketing campaign have included: sponsoring the runaway TV success *Big Brother*, as well as sponsoring Channel 5's evening movies; linking with established web sites such as Ask.co.uk as well as the popular *Big Brother* site; developing an above-the-line campaign using TV and radio to promote the range of products available and the benefits of shopping online; using advertorials in national magazines and daily papers designed as pull-out-and-keep online shopping guides; and using outdoor advertising media in London for a major poster campaign.

Perhaps the most interesting point to note is that this approach is grounded in an understanding of ShopSmart. com's business aims, its market and customers, eschewing gimmickry or technology for its own sake. These techniques are not particularly unusual, but their approach does emphasise clear design and a down-to-earth, straightforward approach that is often lacking in online businesses.

Data mining and the profit-driven online business

One value of the Internet is the opportunity it provides to capture and use information relating to every customer transaction. The key to effective market segmentation online, and indeed to enabling the profit-driven e-business to customise its web site for the convenience of customers and suppliers, is the concept of data mining, a fundamental requirement for a profitable e-business. There are many examples of the successful application of online data

> **KEY CONCEPT**
>
> Data mining covers the tasks of accessing and leveraging information that a company has gathered on its customers and products, to generate competitive advantage. It has three key components: collecting, analysing and using market information.

mining: Internet retailers such as Amazon.com and eToys.com are classic examples of businesses using data to customise their business services. Dell.com uses information from its sales to ensure that future offers are compelling and competitive, and at the last report its web site generated revenues of $15 million per day.

Airline reservation systems are another good example of the power of data mining, as all major airlines now use large, sophisticated databases to enhance their marketing, sales and customer service. This is all the more remarkable when one considers that a specific airline database is likely to be accessed by thousands of people worldwide making bookings for air travel.

You can be sure that online your competitors will be mining data about your customers – and using it to compete against you. The solution is therefore to act first, be thorough and ensure that you *collect, analyse* and *use* information from your web site.

Collecting information from your web site

Many businesses use computer tools and sophisticated applications so that they can drill down into their customer database and find out a wide range of detailed information. However, this requires a number of steps to ensure success.

1 Decide what information you need to collect and which metrics will be important

It is important to construct a web site that generates opportunities to gather as much customer information as possible, but this needs to be *prioritised* so that the critical information is collected first. Also, there is a danger of collecting too much detail: either the customer will be overwhelmed or your business will be! Furthermore, it is important to understand the conclusions that may be developed from the data, and whether more than one area of information needs to be assessed before conclusions can be drawn. This inter-relation of information is important when analysing data that has been aggregated from a range of sources.

However, the focus for information collection needs to be how to build better, one-to-one relationships with each individual customer. With data mining, the name of the game is really to provide a customer-based engine that will dynamically drive the development of the web site so that customers receive a continuously improving – and impressive – service.

2 Understand how best to collect the data you require

This process is fundamental, and rather than simply asking questions on your web site, data collection requires a much more sophisticated approach. It may take the form of a few simple, easy-to-answer questions, but these need to be asked at the right time (i.e. when a customer has decided to buy and is at the order screen, give them payment options asking how they would prefer to pay, or whether they would be prepared to pay a premium for delivery). Competitions are another popular method of gathering data, as are online surveys. Pull-down menus not only provide customers with choices and options for their benefit and ease, but highlight customer preferences as well as areas to avoid for the business.

Case Study: Developments in mass-market retailing

Another popular technique is customer loyalty pro-grammes. These highlight a key feature of data collection: the need to gather aggregated data about the preferences and habits of groups of customers, as well as individual data about separate customers' preferences. Of these, individual data is more powerful and can be used to build a customised and compelling offer for every single client.

Interestingly, the club card schemes favoured by many supermarket chains exploded in popularity, only to become yet another source of competition that is now being largely rejected, as supermarkets seem to be focusing their resources on the potential of online shopping customers. The UK food retailer Tesco, which launched Tesco Direct, is an example of a chain that is not only able to innovate, add value and compete in serving its customers through the online medium, but crucially can also *get to know its customers better* using the Internet. Tesco's action here is not unique, and one of the key determinants of succcess is the company's ability not only to refine its online offering, but to use the information to enhance its offline business as well. Time will tell if this innovation translates into greater market share and profitability; more likely, it is a strategy for survival. In the current retail industry it seems to be the case that successful innovation brings survival, while unsuccessful innovation or inaction spells disaster.

3 Test the effectiveness of your web site for data collection

The process of data collection may seem sensible and logical to the business, but it is essential to view it online from the customer's perspective. Are customers simply being asked questions that to them are time consuming, annoying or simply mystifying? If so, you may get a little of the data you require, but at the cost of disaffected customers. Also, there may be obvious questions (such as 'how can we improve our service to you?') that are simply going unasked – so consider the obvious before attempting to be too clever! The tendency to over-complicate or ask too many questions is a common failing of many web sites.

4   Ensure that the information collected is kept up to date

It is tempting to rely on historical data; while it may occasionally be useful to review the development of trends over time, it is much more important to ensure that data is current and accurate. Achieving this requires a process for ensuring that information is kept up to date. Speed and flexibility are offered by the Internet, expected by the customer and are a positive source of competitive advantage for the business. The profit-driven business therefore needs to be able to act swiftly after receiving information from individual customers, and this needs to be reflected in the construction of the web site and the organisation of the business as a whole.

5   Implement the necessary technology and database systems

As a general rule, all of the transactional information from a web site should be stored in a single database. This enables different departments to draw from a single source, so that production (and suppliers) know exactly what is required and when, and marketing knows who is visiting the web site and ordering, and hence the effectiveness of its efforts to generate traffic to the site. Sales people can know how many customers are repeat purchasers and how many are new. Sales professionals can understand how much traffic is being generated, both into and out of the site, and can then price banner advertising accordingly, for example.

The database selected depends on the size, needs and knowledge of your business, and many businesses that already possess databases developed within the last few years will find that these can probably be extended to include web-based applications. However, this first collection phase is vital in ensuring that the necessary data is collected and held, at the right time and in the most accessible form.

Analysing information from your web site

Analysis falls into two categories: individual and aggregated data. Database vendors provide tools that allow businesses to analyse their activities, with information gathered from a database using a query. This process can be automated for large businesses that routinely need to be able to analyse or respond to information quickly, perhaps across a large volume of customer records (airline reservation systems or online bookstores being prime examples). Furthermore, queries can be combined using 'and' or 'or' commands to identify complex relationships within sets of data; this in turn can be used to identify key issues, opportunities, concerns and trends.

Using customer data

The value of detailed market and customer information is enormous. Common uses of online customer data include:

- *Identifying and tracking customer buying habits* – clickstream technology, showing the path that a customer takes through the web site, will highlight the point at which the customer decides to buy or leaves the site altogether. Tracking customer purchases can also show how frequently customers buy, how much they spend, how they choose to make their purchase and, perhaps most importantly, what they are choosing to buy. This information about customers' buying preferences is the place to start when building an on-going, online relationship with customers, enabling your business to target its products profitably at the customers most likely to buy them.

- *Enhancing the effectiveness of special offer promotions* – for example, by understanding that many customers buying family holidays online also buy a specific type of travel insurance, means that a travel web site can offer these products as a package. It is able to present them to those customers that need them (i.e. those buying family holidays) rather than those that do not. Crucially, analysis of web site data can reveal that the business does not need to discount the price of travel insurance to customers buying family holidays. This can remove 'wasted' margin that may occur when the price of a product is reduced to attract people who would be prepared to buy at the higher price, as well as ensuring that the people who would value the offer are the ones hearing about it.

- *Maximising sales opportunities, leading to repeat business and increased revenue at marginal cost* – closely linked with the previous benefit of more effective special offer promotions is the ability to increase customer response rates through improved targeting, driving an increase in sales. This can occur when a customer who is a current or potential buyer of one type of product is targeted with a complementary product. For example, if a customer is viewing cars, an advertisement for a financing package may appear. Another example is a supermarket that sells online: when a customer is looking at pasta, an advertisement for olive oil and tomato sauce appears. These ads can be targeted by demographics. Using customer data in this way significantly increases marketing effectiveness, and product offers such as this can be used to drive traffic and direct customers to the products that they want – and that you want to sell!

- *Developing new sources of revenue online* – the previous examples show that ads can be used to increase the effectiveness of your business. This not only works to benefit your customers directly, but it can also be used to provide direct benefits for you from your suppliers. To take the example of the online travel agency, it may consider charging a commission to the insurance company providing travel insurance for families, on the grounds that the agency can provide direct access to the insurer's target audience at exactly the right moment to make the sale. Detailed customer data may also highlight new, unknown or previously difficult-to-exploit business opportunities. The online travel agency may have avoided selling ancillary products, from insurance to sun cream, but given the potential new scale of its business and the ability to sell ever more effectively to a wider range of people within the target market, product extensions may prove worthwhile. Another opportunity to consider is the ability to sell space on your web site. However, to achieve maximum advantage, target the right partners and price this effectively, it is often necessary to be able to provide detailed information about the type and frequency of customer visits.
- *Developing new ways to bond with customers* – increasing customer satisfaction and adding value in customer relationships are important sources of competitive advantage. These opportunities are explored further in the rest of this chapter and techniques for developing customer loyalty online are outlined in Chapter 7, Building brands and customer loyalty.

Harnessing the power of the Internet to develop business markets

As technology continues to develop more and more quickly, even relatively recent marketing systems and innovations start looking dated and become obsolete: in other words, they simply fail to deliver their full potential unless they are constantly updated. Yet at the same time technology is enabling businesses to rediscover the levels of service and customer intimacy of a bygone age, and the most successful firms are those that can adapt and profit from this knowledge by harnessing technology.

The most significant advantages of the Internet for marketers are focused on the ability to open up new relationships with customers. These benefits include:

- *Capturing, storing and disseminating information* in unparalleled detail about customer preferences. This in turn supports swift and effective decision making on everything from product development and pricing strategies to stock levels and future marketing plans.
- *Speeding up the rate at which transactions are made,* as well as improving the reliability of these transactions, has both created efficiencies and reduced costs.
- *Examining current and potential relationships between decisions and outcomes,* effectively modelling different scenarios and greatly enhancing the speed and accuracy of decisions.
- *Combining and manipulating a wide variety of different sources of information,* such as the tacit knowledge of employees or market research data, to measure and refine marketing effectiveness and profitability, usually through improved targeting.
- *Enabling special offer promotions* that are sophisticated and offer significant value. As well as facilitating the running of the promotion in the first place, IT also enables

customer data resulting from loyalty schemes and special offer promotions to be thoroughly analysed, with the results used to inform future decisions.

Using the Internet to measure market trends and enhance flexible decision making

The Internet is an invaluable tool for driving sales and profitability, whether it is being used to bond with customers and build loyalty, to improve the customer's knowledge of products and services, or to leverage a sense of market developments (a concept known as market sensing). Knowing what customers want has always been a pre-condition of a successful business, but now more than ever the key to competitiveness online is to know what *each individual customer* wants. There are many ways in which the profit-driven e-business can use the Internet to understand more about markets and customers, and some of the key methods are detailed below.

Analysing customer data from loyalty schemes and special offer promotions helps to enhance the value of loyalty schemes for customer bonding. For example, a growing number of retailers have formed customer clubs, and these have been promoted heavily by supermarkets such as Tesco and Sainsbury in the UK and Migros in Switzerland. Similar to the frequent-flyer programmes offered by airlines, members of customer clubs are rewarded with discounts and special offers for joining and presenting their membership card at every purchase occasion. Not only do retailers benefit by increasing consumers' loyalty, they also collect *individual-level purchase data*. The value of this data to the retailer can be significant. For example, it can calculate which customers account for the greatest proportion of profit.

Manufacturers pay close attention to individual-level data when they have recently introduced a new product, as it can be vital to profitability. Aggregate sales figures may show whether the product is a success at the moment, but the trial rates (percentage of customers who have bought the product once) and repeat rates (percentage of customers who have bought the product at least a second time) available from individual-level data reveal the long-term prospects for the product. Estimates of trial and repeat rates are often used in deciding whether to introduce a product at all and this data can be combined with scanner-level data (from products' barcodes), or in the online environment clickstream data based on analysis of the customers path to, around and from your web site.

Using the Internet to increase flexibility and improve decision making is feasible where brand and product managers use customer data collected via web sites, either directly online or in combination with data from other sources (such as store-level data). For estimates of market share and sales, brand managers are most comfortable with data collected at the store level. All purchases in the store are captured and market research companies that collect this data do a good job of covering most stores in a country.

Using the Internet to build better – and distinctive – relationships with customers

The application of technology to store, analyse and disseminate information is not only providing swifter and more effective methods for decision making, it is opening up new opportunities for building better and more distinctive relationships with customers.

As well as the Internet enabling firms to rediscover long-forgotten levels of service and customer intimacy, technology is helping firms to profit from their greater knowledge. For example, statistical tools are computing the impact on profitability of customer loyalty programmes, where lower

prices reward frequent purchasing. Furthermore, information about customers'
preferences and behaviours
are being captured as businesses utilise technology in
their day-to-day activities.

> **KEY CONCEPT**
>
> For the profit-driven e-business,
> gigabytes of information have
> replaced the shopkeeper's memory
> as a store of knowledge about a
> customer's preferences.

After the introduction of scanner technology to make
transactions much quicker and more reliable, retail stores
have found themselves with enormous databases of transactions that have proved very useful in decision making. As
many transactions migrate to the Internet it is possible not
only to capture purchase data, but also the information that
the customer requested prior to making a choice. As
companies accumulate this data, successful firms will
differentiate themselves from less successful ones by understanding and utilising it to make their enterprises more
profitable.

Using the Internet to measure and refine advertising effectiveness

Transactions taking place on the Web are effortlessly,
economically and automatically recorded, and purchasing on
the Web generally requires the buyer to give personal
information. Typically, the minimum is credit card details and
a postal address, although you may also be asked or required
to fill out a short questionnaire. Even where no purchase is
made, some information may be requested. For example,
newspaper web sites such the *Financial Times* and *The New
York Times*, which are free, ask (at the time of writing) that
you use the same username and password when you visit.
This information can subsequently be used to analyse reading
patterns. How many people only read the headlines, but do so
every day? How many read every article, but visit the site

infrequently? The anonymity of browsing through periodicals at a news-stand does not exist on the Web, and the information recorded can be used by managers to great effect.

Peapod.com, an online supermarket and one of the more sophisticated recorders and users of customers' personal data and shopping behaviour, has led the way in measuring advertising effectiveness. With thousands of customers across the US, Peapod's web site sells groceries that are delivered to customers' homes. A list of previous purchases (including brand, pack size, quantity purchased) is kept on the site, so a customer can make some minor changes from week to week, saving time and effort. Peapod creates a database on each shopper that includes their purchase history, online shopping patterns (how they bought), online attitudinal questionnaires (what they are thinking) and demographic data that it purchases from third parties. A shopper's profile is used to determine which advertisement to show and which promo-tions/electronic coupons to offer. Demographically identical neighbours are thus treated differently based on what Peapod has learned about their unique preferences and behaviours over time.

Shoppers seem to like this high-tech relationship market-ing, with 94 per cent of all sales coming from repeat customers. Manufacturers also benefit, with the more detailed customer information enabling them to target promotions at customers who have repeatedly bought another brand, thereby not giving away promotions to their own loyal customers. This is clearly one of the most significant methods of maximising revenue and reducing costs.

Using your web site to collect and analyse customer information – clickstream data

Given the potential advantages to consumer and vendor alike, the challenge of using your web site effectively is twofold.

First, you need to develop a site that collects the relevant data in an unobtrusive way to which customers won't object; and second, you should determine how to analyse the vast quantity of data that will be collected and integrate it into decision making.

Collecting data online starts when people who visit a site for the first time are asked to register, typically giving a name, physical address, e-mail address and usually some other demographic data (such as age or income). From the customer's perspective this is all that needs to be done. When the site is visited by the same customer in the future, they either type their chosen username and password or the web site recognises the person using a cookie (a small file that uniquely identifies the computer). In either case, each subsequent visit by that customer can be associated with the answers given on the registration form.

> **KEY CONCEPT**
>
> For managers focused on mass production, realising the full potential of the Internet may be difficult. The real key to marketing success and profit growth on the Internet is personalisation: the concept of mass customisation.

Once this process is in place, the manager has to ensure that the web site is personalised for the customer, using as much of the data about them as possible to ensure that the site is appealing and targeted to the interests and needs of that one customer. As the customer repeatedly visits the site, more is learned about them as their series of 'clicks' are recored, the information they request using their mouse. Clickstreams allow the web site to add behavioural information to the answers given at registration.

A successful case of the successful use of clickstream data is CDNow, an online vendor of music CDs. Part of the reason for the success of this business is that it analyses instances where shoppers look at information about a CD but choose not to buy: it is not only purchases that reveal what a person is interested in. Similarly, the web page that a customer sees at the BMG Music Service web site depends on their music preferences and purchase history. Customisation not only improves the relationship with the customer, constant monitoring of the web site also enables marketers to move more quickly to change promotions that are performing poorly.

Understanding the implications of one-to-one marketing via the Internet

The implications of personalisation for consumers are, of course, enormous. Consumers generally do not mind being asked to part with information in order to receive a personalised product or service, and positively value what they perceive as a benefit. However, it is worth keeping in mind the experience of one business that tried to leverage new technology to personalise its service: it went too far and using data collected online, telephoned customers with a sales pitch emphasising a disconcerting amount of personal information. Consumers reacted negatively, offended by what they considered an invasion of privacy.

> **KEY CONCEPT**
>
> In a study by Jupiter Communications, 35 per cent of Internet executives surveyed said that personalisation capabilities were the most important determinant of whom they use to develop their web site.

The implications of personalisation for businesses are far-reaching and will continue to develop as a key driver of strategy, growth and profitability. Companies selling information rather than products over the Internet have been able to charge advertisers more as their advertising becomes more targeted. The amount of Internet advertising has exploded, mostly because of the growth of the Internet itself, but in part because advertisers can get their advertisements viewed by a more specific, targeted group. Treating customers as individuals is continuing to become much more prevalent, and soon it will become just another cost of doing business. The personalisation we see developing on the Internet will have far-reaching consequences in the offline world as consumers' expectations are influenced by their online experiences.

Internet pricing

CHAPTER 5

Overview

It may appear surprising to dedicate an entire chapter to Internet pricing, but this is a vital aspect of achieving business profitability online. The 'wrong' price can undermine an e-business strategy, including its innovation, loyalty building and brand, whereas an effective pricing strategy will support the aims and success of the business immensely. This chapter:

- Outlines the main issues affecting product pricing on the Internet.
- Provides a practical guide to Internet pricing strategies (based on original research).
- Highlights areas to consider when assessing your organisation's success in developing its markets to increase profitability. This last section draws together the key themes of market development that are set out in Chapter 4, and provides an introduction to the Internet selling techniques outlined in Chapter 6.

Issues affecting Internet pricing

The essential points to remember about product pricing on the Internet are outlined below.

Customers' perceptions are a vital consideration when setting prices

In particular, expectations of an Internet price may vary significantly from what applies in the offline environment. If the vendor is offering an enhanced service – and customers understand this – they will typically accept a different price. But the customer cannot be fooled: they will have a view about what justifies a specific price, and they can shop around very easily using the Internet.

> **KEY CONCEPT**
>
> Price very often becomes a key competitive battleground on the Internet. One popular approach is to use a new business model, with new levels of service and value added via the Internet, and an entirely new (and profitable) pricing structure to match.

Price can be used to add value and provide an innovative product offer

Focusing on pricing and profitability can help to redefine business models, highlighting areas where value can be added for the customer. Pricing directly influences customers' perceptions of the product, and a premium price may stimulate sales if it reinforces a customer's perception of quality, prestige or other intangible factors such as reliability. Interestingly, it is these new, intangible factors that are providing the key area of competition on the Internet. With competition becoming ever more intense, there is a premium on adding value.

> **KEY CONCEPT**
>
> An individual's sequence of clicks, called clickstreams, is at the core of personalising web sites. Clickstreams reveal what the customer is really interested in – and what they are not. This can be a vital tool when setting and altering prices.

The classic example of this is the online supermarket, with customers paying a *little* extra for the greater service and convenience of buying online and having the shopping delivered. This service can be enhanced further with a 'smart'

Internet site that develops a tailored shopping list based on a customer's preferences, and offers this each time that the customer logs on to the site.

However, it is important to know how elastic demand is. The key questions used to be: Is the planned innovation possible? Will technology allow it? Now, the more relevant questions are: To what extent is this innovation valued? What is needed to ensure that this increases *profitability*, not simply sales volumes?

Timing is decisive when setting prices

The commercial importance of being a first mover in pricing on the Internet is huge. Many businesses enter online markets – or if they are already established enhance their competitiveness – using price.

The Internet makes pricing transparent

Whereas it used to be possible for a car company to charge widely varying prices in different geographic markets, these are rendered transparent by the Internet. For the customer, the fear is that prices will stabilise at the highest level; while for the vendor, the fear is that prices will be driven down by competition to the lowest level. What normally happens in fact is that businesses use the Internet to innovate and add value, ensuring that purchasing from one online site is significantly different to buying from another, making like-for-like comparisons less useful. However, price transparency may be a driver of change and a key competitive issue to consider when setting prices.

Price can be used to reinforce other areas of e-business strategy

These include brand management, customer base, product position and future product development. Despite the hype and potential offered by the Internet, it is vital to keep in

KEY CONCEPT

Used creatively, price can be a major driver of innovation, competitive advantage and profitability when selling online.

mind the fundamental truths about pricing: it directly affects sales growth; it is a critical determinant of profitability; and it can be difficult to alter once fixed.

GETTING STARTED: issues to consider when pricing on the Internet

- *Monopoly and competitive issues.* The number of competitors and their strategies when selling online should influence pricing. For example, a large number of competitors may focus your business on finding ways to add value, redefining the market; or it may encourage you to focus on a niche or unfulfilled market segment. This is particularly easy to achieve when the rest of the online competition is acting like sheep (a surprisingly frequent phenomenon on the Internet), with broadly the same product and value proposition.
- *The type of market competition.* The type of competitors, their strengths and weaknesses, will also influence pricing. For example, some competitors may be vulnerable to lower prices, as their costs prevent them from lowering prices any further; this is particularly the case where competitors are in different countries. Other competitors may be open to claims of poor value or quality, and in this scenario a higher price accompanied by an appropriate advertising campaign could reinforce perceptions of your product's premium value and quality. The key here is to target one competitor, or one group of competitors, and to attack them with the most appropriate pricing strategy.

♦ *Price elasticity of demand,* how the volume of demand is influenced by changes in price. When demand is elastic, total earnings increase as prices fall (and total earnings fall if prices rise). When demand is inelastic, earnings rise and fall with prices. Elasticity of demand can be calculated as the percentage change in the volume of demand, divided by the percentage change in price. Price elasticity is expressed as a number greater than one; when elasticity is less than one, demand is said to be inelastic. The value of elasticity of demand is in its effect on volumes and total earnings, and calculations of revenue need to take this into account.

♦ *Supply and demand.* Generally, when supply exceeds demand, prices will fall. This has happened most notably in recent years in the oil industry, but it is a fact that often affects most commodities and resources. The converse is also true: when demand exceeds supply, prices will rise, and a key element in marketing strategies is often to stimulate demand by 'creating' a perception of scarcity. High-level advisers, including consultants, lawyers and accountants, are examples where demand often exceeds supply, and the best ones charge the most on the basis that they are at the top of the pyramid – so good that there are relatively few around.

♦ *The nature of the customer.* This is one of the biggest issues underlying Internet pricing: what the customer *wants* and *expects.* Successful pricing and marketing strategies can be devised using the Internet, by researching, questioning and adapting products to see that they meet the needs of each individual customer.

♦ *The culture of the market.* If there is an acceptance of a particular type of pricing structure or approach, strategies will often follow this. The opportunity therefore exists to break the mould, adding value to the product or service offer or simply deciding not to offer it in a certain, established way, but perhaps using the innate advantages of the Internet to develop a new, better and differently priced offer.

◆ *Development, production and distribution costs.* The product's costs are a critical factor when setting prices. A product can, of course, be sold at a loss, for example to establish market share, drive out competitors or build an installed base, but this should always be a conscious decision! Break-even analysis is a valuable method for setting prices or calculating risk. In essence, the likely costs are calculated and divided by the proposed price: if the outcome is an unfeasibly high or low volume of sales, the price needs to be re-examined, as well as expectations of sales volumes.

◆ *Product portfolio.* Pricing is a useful tool for differentiating between products, and there are several reasons for wanting to use pricing in this way:
- to position a product alongside the rest of a business's portfolio so that its offerings are complementary or comprehensive;
- to establish a position for the product in its market, relative to its competitors;
- to build or reinforce a brand image or reputation.

Effective Internet pricing strategies

There is a range of pricing strategies suiting a variety of circumstances. The key is to remember that one price set at one time must usually bear some relation to another set at another time *as far as the customer is concerned* – and always to keep the customer's position clearly in mind. This can make it quite difficult to change quickly between pricing strategies.

The survey outlined in Table 5.1 is based on a broad analysis of 100 web sites during 2000 and in-depth discussions with online marketers.

Table 5.1: Survey of pricing strategies

Pricing strategy	About the strategy	Making it work online
1 Loss leading Selling a product at less than its cost to remove competitors or to establish market share. Internet usage: high Risk: high	This is an age-old, high-risk strategy used when established businesses (with deep pockets) move into the online environment, or when start-ups aggressively attack competitors to establish their presence. It has led to massive market valuations for many online businesses, yet with little or no profit. In effect, companies are betting on their ability to retain customers as they start increasing prices.	Loss leading is a polarising tactic – businesses either love it or hate it – and it can sometimes even become a desperate tactic. It can work online but it is risky. If demand rises too far too fast – an easy occurrence with e-commerce trading – so do the product's losses. Conventionally, it can also be a trap from which there is no easy escape, as customers expect low prices and may even resent them being increased. The same is true online. To make it work online you must: 1 Ensure from the outset that it is part of a specific strategy with targets, deadlines and contingencies in place. 2 Monitor developments – and losses. 3 Have a reason for starting to charge or for increasing prices that is customer based. Added value, content or an enhanced service may be valid reasons in the eyes of the customer; the fact that you can no longer afford the strategy will probably not be! 4 Consider including your customers in the strategy, telling them when you will start charging, or charging more, and crucially explain to them why.
2 Penetration pricing Combining a low price with aggressive marketing to penetrate the market, rapidly establish a presence and gain market share. Internet usage: high Risk: high	Another high-risk strategy particularly suited to entering competitive markets online or attacking established leaders in a specific market. The hope is that as demand rises unit costs will fall and the whole exercise will prove profitable. The danger is that competitors will reduce their prices, so if possible it is best to do it when competitors' prices are already low.	Again, this tactic needs to be part of a broader pricing and market-entry strategy. Online as elsewhere, price advantages tend to prove popular for a while but then other key factors – such as service or product features – tend to rival it in importance. To adopt this approach successfully it can be useful to: 1 Be clear about the role of pricing in the overall marketing strategy. 2 Be able to sense or determine when – at exactly what point in time – prices need to rise. 3 Be aware how this rise in price will be presented to each customer. 4 Know to what extent a future rise in price will affect volumes and profits.

■ **Table 5.1:** (continued)

Pricing strategy	About the strategy	Making it work online
3 Price differentiation Charging variable prices for the same product in different markets, usually according to what customers are willing to pay. Internet usage: low Risk: low for physical products where product factors (such as shipping) may be significant; high if the customer does not understand or agree with the need for a differential	Conventionally, this strategy enables the business to generate the most revenue from its product; however, it has its risks. It only works when there are barriers to entry such as tariffs or high transport costs that prevent wholesalers buying in low-price markets and reselling. It also relies on a measure of consumer ignorance – or tacit acceptance – of prices elsewhere.	This strategy is unusual online because the Internet is a global medium: whether you are buying from an executive suite in Manhattan or a village in a developing country, the price and benefits are apparent for all to see. To make it work effectively you should consider: 1 Providing differentiated prices for other market sectors, such as industries, and not merely different geographic markets. 2 Providing different versions of the same product as a means of justifying price differentiation. Online, this may simply mean newer, more up-to-date products. 3 Whether to add product or service features to an item to support differentiation. 4 Having an excuse ready for those customers who don't understand why they should pay more. (And, given high-speed communication in the online environment, customers will always find out!)
4 Milking or skimming Charging premium prices for top-quality versions of an established, standard product. Internet usage: medium Risk: medium	This involves selling an established product to a high-income market, and convincing that market of the advantages over the standard version. Examples online would be a supermarket providing an at-home delivery service for a professional high-end market.	Although this is typically a low-risk strategy, the danger online is that greater costs can combine with a smaller market, making this approach of limited value. It is therefore vital to ensure the following: 1 The market for this approach is clearly understood and sized. 2 The approach is marketed effectively, and online this means ensuring that marketing is targeted almost on a one-to-one basis, with detailed customer information used to improve the effectiveness of the communication. 3 The approach is clearly differentiated from other products or services, preventing confusion from arising. 4 The benefits of buying online are clearly understood and accepted by the customer.

▌ Table 5.1: (continued)

Pricing strategy	About the strategy	Making it work online
		5 The approach is thoroughly costed: online developments can require a significant investment to ensure success, and premium prices online usually need to reflect higher costs as well as higher potential margin. Detailed market research online is without exception invaluable in making this approach a success.
5 Target pricing The business targets the minimum level of profits that it wants to generate, estimates likely sales volumes at specific prices and fixes the price accordingly. Internet usage: high (especially among established businesses migrating from the offline environment) Risk: low to medium	This is the conventional and most universally adopted approach to pricing (certainly in the offline world), but it does rely on accurate estimates of sales volumes and it can tend to ignore competitors' actions.	One of the greatest risks in adopting this approach online is of over-shooting or under-shooting the market potential, the actual market size and likely response of customers and competitors. The key to managing and reducing risk therefore lies, as with so much about the Internet, in asking and testing before committing. Key areas to focus on with target pricing online are: 1 Preparing estimates of likely sales volumes (adopting worst- and best-case scenarios can be useful). 2 Fixing costs and ensuring that whatever the sales volumes, there is still a positive balance between cost and price. 3 Considering how to build in flexibility and change pricing. The Internet environment demands speed of response and flexibility, so planning to reduce costs and prices may be one approach, and product innovation, adding value to service and increasing volumes by marketing to new sectors may also be areas on which to focus.
6 Marginal cost pricing Charging a price that reflects the extra cost of supplying one extra item to the customer. Internet usage: low Risk: medium to high	This approach works best when the costs of one extra item vary significantly (for example, postage or parcel delivery rates varying according to location). However, it does require an explanation of why	Clearly, this pricing strategy works in certain markets and with specific products, although its use tends to be restricted to the business-to-business environment. The great weakness of this approach at any time is its lack of customer focus, although admittedly for certain items (such as commodities) this may not be too significant. It is therefore important

Table 5.1: (continued)

Pricing strategy	About the strategy	Making it work online
	prices vary for what is essentially the same item. Online, its use is limited as other, generally more imaginative and customer-focused strategies are adopted.	to understand the nature of the market and whether there are opportunities to use price in an innovative way, before simply taking a cost-based approach to pricing. An interesting online variation of this approach was the decision in 2000 by the best-selling author Stephen King to sell his new book exclusively via the Internet, priced at a dollar per chapter. This removed the traditional mediating role of the publisher and was, by all accounts, very successful and profitable. This approach highlights the possibilities of developing innovative online pricing.
7 Variable pricing Prices are reduced to stimulate business, and prices are raised to deter business (if production capacity is full, for example). Internet usage: medium Risk: medium	This is a popular tactic both to stimulate demand when sales are low and to deter it when sales are too high.	The danger of this approach is in explaining to customers about the price fluctuations, and particularly why a reduced price must now rise. When adopting this approach, therefore, it is important to: 1 Add value – possibly as a test or to give the customer a reason for returning to the site – so that there is a rationale as far as the customer is concerned for fluctuating prices. 2 Understand the price elasticity of the market: for instance, in the fast-moving environment of Internet pricing, will a price rise that is intended to be temporary lead to a general decline in popularity of the site from which the business will struggle to recover? 3 Bear in mind the competitive situation of the market and if possible develop a flexible pricing strategy based around product development and improvement.
8 Average cost pricing Calculating total costs and desired profit margin, and dividing this total by likely sales volumes to set a base price.	This is one of the most popular approaches to pricing and is most readily accepted by customers. It relies on accurate estimates, but it has the advantage of enabling firms with the	This approach relies heavily on estimates of sales volumes and costs, and online these can be particularly vulnerable areas for established and new businesses alike. It tends to works best where the product is information, for example with banks or newsletter publishers that are delivering their

Table 5.1: (continued)

Pricing strategy	About the strategy	Making it work online
Internet usage: medium Risk: low	lowest costs to charge the lowest prices.	product online. It is less successful where the product has to be delivered, for example a music CD, unless that product (i.e. the music) can also be delivered online in a format that meets customers' needs. Achieving success therefore requires: 1 Accurate research into market size and costs. 2 Measures in place to monitor market trends, so that changes in volume and cost are foreseen in time. 3 An ability to use pricing to drive product innovation – for example, music CD's able to be sold and delivered online.
9 Customary pricing Charging the same price but reducing the contents of the package. Internet usage: medium Risk: medium to high	This approach – which can be viewed as almost immoral in the offline world – is quite acceptable online, often because of the crucial element of convenience.	The danger is that this approach will simply become an attempt to increase profits by tacitly misleading customers, occurring when costs are rising and demand is slow. Clearly, the risk is resentment by the customer. To make this approach work online you need to: 1 Understand why customers will buy a product that is reduced in content, at the same price. This may be as an add-on to a new product, because the product is at or near the end of its useful life or, best of all, because some of the product features are now so compelling that a higher price can be charged. 2 Communicate with customers.
10 Barrier pricing Reducing prices to deter or remove new entrants to the market. Internet usage: high Risk: high	This can happen in highly competitive or price-sensitive markets, which many online environments (such as bookselling) are. It is an aggressive strategy that works when the company lowering its prices is defending a core market (e.g. an	Reducing prices always carries a risk and, as with all of these strategies, it is important to: 1 Understand customers' needs and likely reactions. 2 Understand how competitors may respond – a classic response to this tactic from competitors is often to maintain their higher price but look to add greater value.

Table 5.1: (continued)

Pricing strategy	About the strategy	Making it work online
	old-economy business entering the online environment without being a first mover). The company taking this approach needs to be wealthy enough to sustain such an approach.	3 Consider how this pricing strategy links with the long-term success of the brand in the market, and whether it can be used to help drive product development, innovation and customer service. 4 Ensure that the approach is part of a broader, clearly understood and long-term pricing strategy. 5 Make the most of the price reduction so that it not only deters or removes new entrants, but opens up new opportunities and markets, ideally increasing web traffic and sales.

Vital questions and answers

. . . when assessing your organisation's success in developing its markets to increase profitability

How effectively do you analyse and refine the effectiveness of marketing programmes? In particular, how effectively do you use the Internet for market sensing and market research?

The Internet has an increasingly important role in market sensing and market research and it is useful to consider the extent to which technology is used to monitor competitors and refine mental models of the marketplace. Because the Internet can easily handle and manipulate large amounts of data, its value in tracking customer preferences and accurately targeting marketing activities is enormous. Consider also the extent to which information systems provide an understanding of

CONTINUED . . . **Vital questions and answers**

business activity at the customer level: for example, who are the largest customers according to sales and profitability? How have these changed over time and why?

How effectively does your business capture and analyse data resulting from loyalty schemes and special offer promotions?

The value of such activities is not only that they build customer loyalty, but that they provide valuable customer information. This includes details about what people want, how they buy, how the product can be improved and how best to market to each individual customer. At the very least, they can help to refine the effectiveness of the loyalty programme and special offer.

How successful is your business in using customer data to drive product pricing and profitability analysis?

Combining data relating to sales volumes with an analysis of pricing can help to sharpen pricing strategies and enhance profitability. Recording and analysing sales volumes and trends is important to maintain the right level of inventory, in the right place at the right time. Further key questions to consider include:

- whether sufficient data is collected at the point of purchase;
- whether it is adequately analysed and used as a basis for future decisions;
- whether it could be improved to deliver greater profitability.

CONTINUED ... **Vital questions and answers**

How successful and dynamic is your web site?

Many businesses rush into developing an Internet presence, concerned that they will become marginalised if they do not. However, along with presence must come the other key to success on the web – personalisation. Some of the issues to consider, therefore, include the extent to which the web site is relevant, attractive and up to date. For example, does it collect all of the data that it could, and does it do so in a way that reinforces rather than undermines the brand and does not dismay or upset the customer? What customer benefit does the web site deliver? (Increasingly this is personalisation or speed of service.) This not only means capturing purchase information but clickstream data as well, which can highlight those factors influencing a potential customer's decision to purchase or not.

It is also important to understand how well the site is integrated into the organisation in general, and where the centres of marketing and decision making lie. It may be helpful to review:

- how well it is advertised;
- whether links with other sites could strengthen it;
- whether any elements of the web site would benefit from being outsourced.

What is your pricing strategy online and how effectively does it relate to your business priorities (e.g. gain market share, establish new products or remove and deter competitors)?

When developing your online pricing strategy, it is important to consider how well it supports your overall objectives, such as:

CONTINUED ... **Vital questions and answers**

- how the market – meaning customers and competitors – will react;
- how flexible and adaptive it is if market conditions shift;
- the extent to which it enables you to use price as a source of innovation, not only driving revenue but achieving other advantages such as enhanced customer loyalty and repeat business;
- in what direction it is taking your e-business (mass player or niche provider?).

The next chapter looks further at techniques for developing markets, putting together many of these issues and focusing on the key elements of a dynamic Internet sales strategy.

Developing an Internet sales strategy

CHAPTER 6

Overview

Developing the sales potential of your business is perhaps the greatest challenge and opportunity of the Internet. However, this potential brings with it a range of complex problems, including:

- understanding and focusing on customer needs in this radically new sales environment;
- competing, when competitors may often have pockets deep enough to run their Internet activities at a loss;
- reorganising your business so that it is prepared and structured internally for success.

One successful approach is to redefine the market on your terms: the old rules may no longer apply and a new reality can be created that suits your business, providing a profitable source of competitive advantage. The techniques to achieve this are outlined in this chapter, which explains:

CONTINUED . . . Overview

- the benefits of selling on the Internet and the requirements for a successful Internet sales strategy;
- techniques for effectively selling – and closing – using the Internet.

Selling on the Internet: an overview

Internet selling – the positive approach

KEY CONCEPT

Adopting a positive but realistic attitude is vital the success of your Internet sales strategy. Businesses can be damaged both internally (lower levels of morale and innovation, staff leaving) as well as externally (more open to competitors or simply missing customers' expectations) if the Internet selling strategy is ill conceived or poorly motivated – and hence likely to fail.

Selling is frequently seen as the killer app, the greatest benefit and, frankly, the main reason for embracing (or battling with) the complexity of the Internet. It is important to consider for a moment the issues driving Internet selling for companies. For some it is the massive opportunity that drives developments: the opportunity to reach a global market of millions, to achieve market dominance, enter new markets, launch new products, compete. In other words, it is a positive strategy.

If this is driving your approach, then a word of warning: many businesses can, have and will lose money by not following through on the *detail* of their Internet sales plans, either in the strategic-level planning or the detailed execution. For example, many Internet venture capitalists highlight issues of financial expectations when assessing bids for venture capital, and while it is true that this could apply to any business start-up, it is a salutary reminder of the days of unrealistic expectations, investments, capitalisations and crashes that started to capture the headlines from late 2000 onwards.

A businessperson may outline a strategic plan with the triumphant claim that their business will take a 50 per cent share of a $1 billion-a-year market. On closer inspection, however, many customers in this market may not use the Internet and other market conditions will often significantly reduce the actual Internet market potential, perhaps to $200 million a year. If the new business gains a 50 per cent share of this market (an ambitious plan), revenues will be $100 million. If direct trading costs and overheads are removed this would typically, for many industries, provide a yield of 15 per cent net margin, or $15 million a year – and this excludes Internet start-up costs. That is a far cry from the expectations that dominating a $1 billion business might generate.

Some lessons highlighted by this, albeit very rudimentary, analysis:

- A billion-dollar market is not big – and for the Internet you need to think big.
- The devil is in the detail – don't be seduced by numbers and forecasts on spreadsheets, plan for the worst.
- Assess and clearly understand the market – how it works and what makes your approach so compelling, unique and widely understood.
- Focus on finances and costs – not only can they escalate, they can be high to begin with. And web sites, with their associated costs of staffing, maintenance, development and promotion, cost money.

Internet selling – the negative approach

An alternative approach is to be cautious. Many people are resentful of the Internet, which for many reasons can be seen as intrusive, over-hyped, ineffective, even irrelevant. The reason that such executives 'get on the Web' is because they are told to, or simply because they feel they may be missing out at some stage in the future. There are a number of potential pitfalls with this approach:

- *The culture of the Internet relies on flexibility and dynamism.* Simply getting on the Web is not enough; it's about as useful as entering the television broadcasting market with a radio programme and it will positively harm your Internet strategy.

> **KEY CONCEPT**
>
> Many businesses rush the development of their Internet selling strategy, often in a competitive, media- (or supplier-) driven frenzy to 'get on or miss out'. As with any major new development, assess what you want to achieve, whether the time is right and how the potential of the Internet to boost sales will be realised.

- *A sales approach that is reluctant,* overly contrived or in any sense negative is usually doomed to failure.
- *If external market conditions are not right,* if it is not appropriate, then wait. This might be the case, for example, with a business selling to a market without a need or acceptance of computers (from street vendors to developing-country sharecroppers). Furthermore, current Internet take-up on a national scale varies widely, even within Europe, and while it is set to increase, even during a potential economic downturn, the level of demand and overall potential will still be patchy.
- *Internet selling fails when it is perceived, internally or externally, as an 'add-on'.* It needs to be embraced by the business as a whole and will certainly make demands across the whole business. Integration is therefore vital to Internet selling success.
- *Timing and competitiveness are critical success factors.* Internet selling may be an opportunity, but resources may be better spent focusing on existing channels – although the danger here is of an Internet start-up 'reinventing' your market and leaving you behind.

How the Internet can benefit your organisation's sales activities

Using the Internet to sell provides many advantages, not simply the obvious ones of connecting with more customers across a wider spectrum. Understanding these advantages is useful for getting to grips with the nature of Internet selling in general and the potential for your organisation in particular. The key benefits are:

- increasing sales;
- reducing sales costs;
- satisfying customers so that they return (and also leave competitors);
- gaining market share and competitive advantage by reinventing whole industries.

Increasing sales

Before discussing the potential of Internet sales, it is useful to understand *how* the Internet can be used to develop sales.

- *Enabling you to sell everywhere, all the time.* Known as 24/7 Internet access, this means your business is always available to sell as well as communicating with your customers, constantly adding value. The goal is often to make your business the easiest and most accessible to do business with.
- *Closing more sales.* An amazing 75 per cent of Internet shopping carts are abandoned, meaning that most Internet shopping transactions are uncompleted. The challenge here is therefore to encourage users to complete their purchases, not only with a compelling offer but also by guiding them through the sales process, providing customer-focused support and accurate information at every step.

- *Increasing your average order size.* This is a significant achievement indeed at a time when the absolute number of orders is also rising. However, this can be accomplished by using the data from Internet transactions to focus – and closely target – up-selling and cross-selling opportunities.
- *Selling additional products (either add-ons or launching new product lines).* Customer data from the Internet can be used to sell new products and product extensions. This can be achieved quickly, often during the initial sale, and valuable customer data can be segmented and focused to each individual customer's needs.
- *Improving sales techniques and spreading best practice.* An efficient Internet sales system lends itself to learning and continuous improvement. The best, most effective sales practices can be spread quickly among the rest of the sales force, worldwide.

Reducing sales costs

The Internet enables sales personnel to have the latest, most up-to-date information to help them sell. This might include product information, testimonials, details of special offers, customer or market intelligence. This is particularly valuable for situations

> **KEY CONCEPT**
>
> The Internet ensures that in-depth product information is readily available to the people who can make best use of it, be they sales professionals, distributors, suppliers, key influencers (from journalists to analysts and professional advisers) or customers.

where in-depth product information is needed, and it can be provided directly to distributors and customers, as well as the sales force. However, in reality, to use this information to greatest effect it is probably necessary to provide it via an intranet.

The Internet gives people the chance to view and evaluate products quickly and easily, without assistance, and this can be particularly valuable for complex products or rapidly evolving markets. As a result, product and technical experts can be used for greater value-added activities. Furthermore, if the sales system is set up effectively, it is possible for complex, customised price quotations to be prepared for customers, possibly without sales people intervening. This has a number of clear advantages: providing an immediate response to customers' enquiries; reducing the lead time for sales; ensuring accurate handover of order details; and saving time and effort in taking and transmitting orders – in effect, doing it better, quicker and much more cost-effectively.

Accuracy is worth focusing on in greater detail as it is another hidden benefit of the Internet. It not only increases speed but leads to great reductions in wastage. Furthermore, depending on the industry and product, it can lead to reductions in inventory costs as products are made to order. All of this can be leveraged for the next benefit of Internet selling, the opportunity to enhance customer loyalty.

Building customer loyalty

The Internet makes it easier to achieve three key elements of customer loyalty: attracting customers (usually by simplifying the process of customers doing business with you), satisfying your customers and keeping them coming back to you. Furthermore, these can all be accomplished at a fraction of their normal cost, and by building greater customer loyalty, sales costs will often be reduced.

 **GETTING STARTED:** using your web site to build customer loyalty

Customers will come back to your web site if they feel comfortable and believe it is relevant to their needs.

However, much more needs to be done with your web site to develop customer loyalty. Customers need to feel that the web site meets the following characteristics:

♦ Simple, helpful and intuitive – easy to use.
♦ Responsive – listening to the customer and understanding what they want without marching them along a predetermined course. (This can be bad enough when a flesh-and-blood sales person does it, when a computer steers you in an unwanted direction it is particularly annoying!)
♦ Accurate as well as immediate, offering the chance to question or change choices before confirming details, without worrying that the service will be incorrect.
♦ Valuable and able to offer an element of service that cannot be found elsewhere.
♦ Delivering a fast and efficient service, with options that are likely to suit the target customer.

If these elements can be included in your web site, the likelihood is that returned shipments, adjustments and dissatisfied customers will decrease, and with this reduction in cost will come an increase in customer loyalty.

Creating new business models

The connectivity of the Internet – combined with technological developments and a measure of innovative, entrepreneurial spirit – can be used to reinvent your business. Being connected to your customers, distributors, personnel and key stakeholders will ensure that you can radically alter the way that you operate. How this can best be achieved for your business needs to be clearly assessed, preferably by as many people within the organisation as is feasible. Given the power and scope of the Internet, it is often the case that *anyone* within the organisation can generate useful ideas about how best to use it to greatest advantage. The following ideas may provide a useful starting point:

KEY CONCEPT

A range of benefits and opportunities arise from Internet selling, but some of the greatest benefits are specific to particular industries, products or organisations. It is therefore worth assessing how your business can apply these techniques and use the Internet to *generate value* for customers in the sales process.

- *Information interchange* – how can buyers and sellers be linked in new and ever more useful ways that will be of value to both sides?
- *Pricing* – this can be a valuable source of innovation and value for the customer, for example by using online auctions or dynamic discounts based on sales information held on IT systems. How can your business innovate on price – and, if you don't, what might your competitors do?
- *Competitors* – what are they doing and do their Internet strategies pose a threat to your business? Can the Internet be used to develop unique advantages that are, in effect, barriers to entry for new competitors?
- *Selling* – how can this be developed to reach as wide an audience as possible? Almost every part of the sales process can be changed with the Internet: it is one of the most liberating advantages of technological innovation, and major competitive advantage can be achieved by the business that radically revises the old ways of doing business into new ways that benefit customers.
- *Products* – what new products, and product extensions, can be developed? How can the Internet help in their research, development, production, delivery and launch? Involving customers significantly and early is often a key to success.

Case Study: Finding the source of profitable on-line marketing – Blue Nile

Blue Nile is a successful US-based business specialising in the difficult – even hazardous – world of selling jewelry on-line. Some potential pitfalls are obvious: lack of a brand presence in a mature and well-established market is a difficulty most frequently shared by new 'e-tailers'. However, to this must also be added high inventory costs and the whole thorny issue of security: from on-line security for customers looking to pay a significant amount of money, to ensuring that delivery is safe and secure as well as timely.

Despite these significant problems faced from the start of the business, two factors were particularly relevant in ensuring Blue Nile's current – and continuing – success: effective and sustained consumer marketing; and focusing clearly on customer profitability.

Key elements of an effective on-line marketing approach

Blue Nile used the e-commerce boom to try a variety of different sales channels and marketing methods. Significant sums were spent on a coordinated TV, radio and newspaper advertising campaign, as well as on-line advertising and massive direct mail. This had two advantages: establishing the brand and also highlighting which channels were the most cost-effective. By the end of 2000 Blue Nile had halved its marketing costs, yet managed to grow sales by 80 per cent as a result of smaller, cheaper direct mail and targeted email campaigns. In addition, the company worked hard to provide a high level of customer service (commensurate with its products, clientele and customer expectations) that helps

CONTINUED ... Case Study: Finding the source of profitable on-line marketing – Blue Nile

it to generate repeat business and increase the average value per order to over $1,000. One example of this was the company's free, next day delivery service, even for customised jewelry.

The result of this approach for Blue Nile had been steady growth, although the focus for the company crucially remains on growing *gross contribution*, not simply revenues. This clear financial emphasis recently earned Blue Nile a $15 million credit line, enabling it to avoid raising money from the public markets.

Key techniques for selling via the Internet

 IMPLEMENTATION CHECKLIST: seven techniques for a successful Internet selling strategy

The seven techniques are explained in detail in the following pages:

1 *Generate participation, ownership and commitment* within the business generally and among senior managers in particular.

2 *Ensure that your Internet selling strategy is all-embracing,* enhancing existing activities as well as learning from past experience.

3 *Simplify the customer's experience* so that the sales process is more streamlined, with barriers to purchasing removed.

4 *Ensure that your web site is sticky and compelling.* Customers need to remain at your web site when they arrive (known

as 'stickiness') – your competitor is only a click or two away – and you need to ensure that customers come back time and again!

5 *Focus on flexibility and efficient personalisation* so that your customers are empowered to buy exactly what they want, their way.

6 *Avoid duplication and the mistakes of the past*, preventing a complicated, high-cost solution when an effective, low-cost alternative is available.

7 *Plan and prepare internally for the changes that an Internet sales strategy will deliver*, so that you avoid investing too much, too little, too late or too soon.

1 Generate participation, ownership and commitment within your organisation

There are a number of simple guidelines to consider when selling via the Internet. The first is to understand that adopting an Internet sales approach often affects the entire business. Clearly there is an impact on the sales function, but distribution and marketing will also need to review how they can turn the Internet to their advantage, innovating in areas ranging from product presentation, packaging and pricing to special offers and promotions. Beyond this, order processing and fulfilment will need to adapt or change entirely, and service policies will have to change. These are just some of the most frequent changes affecting sales activities; there are many other functions that will need to alter the way in which they work, and this level of cross-functional change requires strong co-ordination, leadership and commitment from senior managers.

For the senior manager, the task is clear: dynamic and empowering leadership is the style that most often succeeds. However, whether you are the senior manager with overall charge, or a manager preparing a case for other senior colleagues, there are several fundamental issues to remember.

Foremost among these is the need to understand your organisation's e-business goals and exactly what you want to achieve. The next step is to agree how to measure success. It is important clearly to define and specify the benefits of the proposed Internet sales system, how they will work in practice and what the outcome will be. Other factors to consider are whether new or existing competitors might gain market share and establish their brands. If it is possible to enter the market, either because there are few barriers to entry or because the business can be redefined, it is as well to know this ahead of time and plan a competitive – and hopefully pre-emptive – response. This last point highlights the dangers of *not* adopting an Internet sales strategy, which need to be considered and understood so that people know the risks and are motivated to change.

2 Ensure that your Internet selling strategy is all-embracing, enhancing existing activities and learning from past experience

There is a clear danger that a new Internet sales strategy will throw the baby out with the bathwater, wiping away existing customer loyalty and damaging brand values that are, and may remain, important. The solution is to assess existing strengths and sales channels and enhance these so that they operate more efficiently. This often means

> **KEY CONCEPT**
>
> Clearly, the best strategy needs to blend past experience and existing resources with the new dynamism and invention of the Internet. One key technique is to use the flexibility of the Internet, testing new approaches and techniques and building on successes. The technology and culture of the Internet allow you to try one approach for a short period before making enhancements.

developing a sales strategy that blends the virtual with the physical presence – often referred to as 'clicks and mortar'. Physical sales channels and retail outlets often complement the Internet presence, with its expanding global reach and 24/7 sales presence. This might enable customers to order via the Internet and choose shipping and delivery options, or it might advise them of the nearest outlet that they can visit to make their purchase.

Another popular approach is to use Internet outlets within existing stores in a way that adds value for the customer. For example, several major retailers provide special offers for customers with loyalty cards, which can be viewed via an online outlet in the store.

3   Simplify the customer's experience

For Internet selling to succeed, it needs to be simple. For the seller, the temptation is to over-complicate, offering too many options, too many distractions. At the start of the twenty-first century, Internet selling is still quite new for many businesses and markets; understanding of what works and what does not in this comparatively new environment is still developing.

 **GETTING STARTED:** simplifying the sales process for the customer

There are a few essential guidelines to consider that will simplify the customer's experience and help you to sell successfully online.

- Helping customers (as well as distributors and sales people) to *navigate easily* through complex products will help convert prospects to sales. This might be achieved with a clear map of the site, explanation of where to find key items or how to ask for help, as well as highlighting new products or innovations. But all the time, keeping the layout clear, attractive and simple is key – and to this can be added the importance of flexibility.

♦ Enable your customers to *move in a seamless flow* through the web site, with simple decisions and preferences included in the process, so that customers can make decisions and express preferences during the process.

♦ Both of these principles require the web site to *simplify the entire sales process*, flowing from initial request (or needs analysis) to product configuration, ordering and delivery.

♦ *Ensure that the web site, or the web provider or developer, is flexible* enough to take account of ways in which your requirements may change and evolve.

♦ *Ensure that your web site is competitive.* To achieve this it needs to provide an experience for the customer that is simple, interactive, engaging and compelling. Uniqueness is also an important attribute, if achievable.

♦ *Consider ways of leveraging knowledge on your web site*, in effect, giving customers access to your information so that they can quickly and easily decide how best to buy. The advantage of this is that it can be a two-way process. It provides you with opportunities to capture and use specific information about each customer (data mining), as well as enabling you to enhance the effectiveness of your web site following the pattern and flow of customers' mouse clicks while online (clickstream data).

4 Ensure that your web site is sticky and compelling

Of course, it is important that customers stay and use your web site, and that they are also happy to return at a later time – the concept of stickiness. Achieving this requires the usual marketing elements of focusing on the customer's need, product offer, pricing, presentation, brand management and other elements, but on the Internet it usually requires two additional elements. First, many of the most successful web sites also provide interesting *content*, something much more than a sales brochure on screen. Second, the site should provide benefits *unavailable anywhere else*. These might be in the form of products, prices, service quality or other differentiators that set it apart from its competitors (these not only include your business competitors but also other channels and offerings that may substitute for your web site).

> **KEY CONCEPT**
>
> In 1998, research indicated that 68 per cent of Internet shopping carts were abandoned, and by 1999 this had increased to 75 per cent. Of these, 31 per cent of customers changed their mind, 26 per cent bought from a competitor and 18 per cent bought offline. Simply put, three-quarters of all customers found the sales process too complex, inconvenient or unconvincing.

It can often help to research and pilot your web site to ensure that these goals are being achieved. It should also be remembered that maintaining a compelling web site requires constant effort, flexibility and expenditure.

5 Focus on flexibility and efficient personalisation

Customers should be empowered to use your web site in a way that suits them best. This means that they should be able to move through the process in an order that meets their needs, while at the same time being guided to a final order. It is worth considering (and knowing!) whether customers find your site:

- easy to locate;
- intuitive, logical, simple to use and interesting;
- helpful – answering all of their queries, or the most likely queries, and providing them with sufficient information to reach a decision (consider including a page of frequently asked questions or FAQs);

- flexible, so that they can roam through it and are able to navigate from almost any point in the buying process.

Flexibility is important. The traditional, offline, linear sales process is frequently inadequate in meeting customers' needs on the Internet. A process that is too rigid may alienate customers, so they should be able to change their minds and back up without having to re-enter information. This also requires that information is instantly available and accurate, and that there are visual cues showing where the customer is in the sales process.

In addition to flexibility, another advantage of the Internet is the ability to build customisation into the sales system. It is worth considering how you might give your customers the greatest flexibility and control of the sales process using the Internet. A classic example of this is the automotive company that enables customers to order the specific type of car they want, with all of the extras listed, priced and ready to order. The customer sits at home reviewing the car company's web site, considering each of the features before deciding whether to buy; in effect, personalising a mass-produced product to their specific needs or requirements. Another example, earlier in the sales process, is the online bookstore that notices when my daughter buys books by a certain author or of a particular genre, and then periodically sends her information relating to her taste in literature. It is worth questioning both *how* your product can be customised and also, separately, *where* in the sales process customisation can be offered.

6 Avoid duplication and the mistakes of the past

Avoiding duplication and mistakes can be achieved with a process of user acceptance testing, checking that users of the system such as customers, partners and suppliers find it to be the best that it could be. Without this, there are the risks of missed opportunities, lack of feedback, stagnation and frustration. These in turn will lead to a lack of ownership and a spiral of inefficiency.

It is also worth completing a risk analysis, assessing where the risks lie in your Internet sales strategy and how these might be overcome. There is a wealth of advice, information and business examples (both successful and less successful), which can be valuable. The costs of an effective Internet sales system can be high and the best web sites, with all the associated costs of re-engineering the business, are usually expensive. However, there is a broad range of commercial software packages that provide excellent Internet sales systems and it may be better to select one of these rather than develop a separate, proprietary package.

Commercial packages may lack a customised fit with your needs, but their benefits can often outweigh this. These benefits include a lower total cost of ownership; a shorter time to market; the ability to focus on your core activities (rather than developing a customised system); the benefit of the vendor's accumulated experience; and the flexibility to take advantage of new technologies and features that may be developed by the vendor.

7 Plan and prepare internally for the changes that an Internet sales strategy will deliver

Preparing for the changes brought about by an Internet sales system involves:

- planning for success;
- integrating systems;
- choosing the right partners.

There is an entertaining television advertisement used by a major parcel carrier and logistics firm, highlighting the importance of preparation for a successful Internet selling strategy. In the ad, a team of excited entrepreneurs are gathered around a computer, one of them presses a key and their new web site goes live. There is a pause and then one order appears on the screen to a round of applause. Suddenly the counter notches up 11 sales, then 75 sales, 200 and then 2,000: the room is cheering and everyone applauds. Then, in the next seven seconds, the number of sales goes from 2,000 to 350,000. The cheering stops. Everyone is stunned into a shocked silence. No one was prepared for this massive level of business.

Clearly, *planning* for success is a frequently overlooked element of Internet selling. It is important to know the number and profile of Internet sales that will be generated so that the business can prepare all aspects of the operation. This starts with the Internet server itself, but goes right to the heart of the order fulfilment system. Many people make the mistake of seeing an

> **KEY CONCEPT**
>
> Effective Internet sales systems rely heavily on *people*. Of course technology matters, but without people delivering the service – and ensuring that the system meets customer needs – there will be no service.

Internet selling system as a technical or technological solution. The emphasis is on the online elements of the system, which are frequently inadequate. What is needed is a holistic approach that incorporates the Internet-based system as a means for meeting customers' needs.

One way to ensure that this is achieved is to plan the *integration* of business systems. There should be a clear process put in place (ideally one that has been tested), which will need to be refined and developed so that:

- the process is easier and ever more convenient and beneficial for the customer;

- it is robust and capable of coping with fluctuations – and growth – in demand;
- people are involved, clearly understanding how they fit into the system and, wherever possible, adding value to the sales process.

For example, what happens if a mistake is made and a customer fails to receive an order? As a general rule, as frustration levels grow so does the desire to talk to a person, not a machine. The same is true in more positive situations, perhaps where a customer wants to become a distributor, or to buy in bulk and discuss special rates. People need to feel ownership of the system in order for them to support and enhance it effectively.

The final element in preparing and delivering a successful Internet sales system is to *choose the right partners*. When selecting a partner it is worth considering what elements matter most to you. If it is customising an order system, that might suggest one partner, whereas if it is supplier management, another partner may be a better bet. Given the growth in businesses providing support capabilities, it is well worth considering in detail what suits your business best.

Building brands and customer loyalty

CHAPTER 7

Overview

New technology is enabling businesses to change the way they think about their markets, customers and products and, in particular, the way they *relate* to their customers. Part of this change is driven by the shift in customers' expectations and part by competitive pressures in general. Issues of service quality and competitive advantage are highlighted in the online environment, and this chapter will cover practical techniques for building customer loyalty to ensure that profits – and shareholder value – increase.

Managing all of these activities in cyberspace is a difficult and demanding task. Accomplished success-fully, it can deliver major advantages; if ignored or inadequately managed, the consequences can be harmful, significant and swift. This chapter will:

- Explore how loyalty drives online profitability and explain practical techniques for developing customer loyalty.

• Outline techniques to ensure that business brands are developed so as to reinforce profits and shareholder value, in the immediate and highly competitive online environment.

Case Study: A fizzing brand, not a bursting bubble – Pepsi.com

One of the most intriguing commercial web sites I have ever seen, existing solely to reinforce the brand among its target market, is Pepsi.com. At first sight the idea of promoting an inexpensive soft drink on the Web seems surprising, possibly a case of an Internet bubble finally bursting. However, the Pepsi approach exhibits a stroke of intelligence and ingenuity that shows how well they know their market – and how effectively they can develop their mass consumer brand online.

Why go online?

The first reason for Pepsi investing in the Internet is, on reflection, obvious: the fit between the brand, the target market and that market's level of Internet penetration is almost perfect. The second reason is Pepsi's position in the market as an innovative brand, a brand perception and personality that can be significantly enhanced through an effective Web presence.

Meeting the challenges of going online

There are many brands that are not looking to sell directly via the Internet, but rather are seeking to

CONTINUED ... Case Study: A fizzing brand, not a bursting bubble – Pepsi.com

reinforce their brand, indirectly boosting sales through offline retail outlets. For these businesses and many others, the critical tension is between developing a fast-moving, entertaining and popular site while also being loyal to the brand, which usually means keeping their focus. Pepsi's original site was provocative and unusual in its tone of voice, almost projecting arrogance, yet it challenged its visitors to participate in 15 online activities, with the winning prize a trip into space worth an estimated $100 000. Pepsi's GeneratioNEXT campaign backed by major pop stars highlighted the popularity of the brand to win over its target market, and so it was logical that these brand values (innovative, ironic, brash, fun) should be reflected in the web site.

For many brands, developing a dynamic site that is also consistently loyal to the brand values can be achieved in the following ways:

- Ensuring that the brand values are known and clearly understood.
- Establishing an unambiguous set of objectives for what the consumer will experience during their visit to the web site (specifically, which part of the brand – such as innovation or prestige – is to be emphasised). These objectives need ideally to be both quantitative and qualitative.
- Researching and verifying these objectives to ensure that they are specific, desirable (both from an external market view and an internal business perspective) and realistic.

CONTINUED ... **Case Study: A fizzing brand, not a bursting bubble – Pepsi.com**

- Developing an action plan that sets out how these objectives will be achieved on the web site and, crucially, *how they will be sustained and developed over time*. The plan therefore needs to be dynamic and time sensitive.

- Developing a marketing plan that is congruent with the position adopted on the site, drives traffic to the site and is implemented at the right time.

- Measuring the value of the web site and refining it further. This can be achieved by assessing the number of individual visitors; the number of repeat visits; the time (in minutes) that each visitor spends on the site, on each specific page and on each activity; the point at which each visitor leaves the site; the point on the site where each visitor lingers longest; the most popular links and the most popular locations for links; the number of e-mails received from visitors and their topics; and, most significantly, the web site's turnover and profitability.

Pepsi.com highlights another vital point: no matter how strong or well known the brand, or how difficult it may be to sell the product directly over the Internet, a brand can always benefit and develop by tapping the potential of a web site effectively. However, the change in Pepsi's web site also shows the need to keep moving, finding different and complementary ways of enhancing the brand, frequently integrating online and offline activities.

How customer loyalty online drives profitability

E-commerce is about customers. Everyone says it, but the successful e-businesses are those that *understand* what that means and know how to deliver what their customers want. Because customer loyalty is accepted as being so fundamental, its impact on profits is rarely examined. There are several key concepts that are important in assessing how customer loyalty feeds profitability online:

- Measuring the profitability of customers.
- Developing a customer's lifetime value to your business.
- Targeting, attracting and retaining the right customers.

Measuring the profitability of customers

There is a tendency to assume that selling online enables a business to increase its potential market size dramatically. The reasons cited for this are twofold: the Internet offers truly global reach; and it is so exciting and compelling that even potential customers outside the normal target group will be interested in buying. The first reason is certainly true, but the second is definitely *not*: online selling relies as much as any other channel on a sound evaluation of customer needs and a clear definition of the target market. While customer retention is best achieved by focusing on each individual customer, it is important to understand who the most profitable customers are, so that this market segment can be dynamically developed.

Measuring the profitability of customers will be of benefit across a range of business activities: it will help to determine the structure, resources, direction and development of the business, but above all it will enable the business continuously to develop and improve its activities. To achieve this, the customer analysis needs to highlight profit per customer, helping to identify the best and least profitable

Table 7.1: Measuring customer profitability

Issues driving customer revenue	Issues driving customer costs
Revenue per customer	Cost per customer (cost of sale as well as total cost per customer)
Number of orders per customer	Cost per order
Referrals from customers	Cost of retaining customers (i.e. cost of loyalty programmes and special offers)
Reasons for not purchasing (or for going to a competitor)	Cost of acquiring a new customer
Future needs and likely volume and value of purchases	Likely (or target) growth and future cost implications
Note: understand the reasons for purchasing, what product/service attributes the customer values most	Note: assess the key drivers of cost and how these can be managed, monitored and controlled

customers. It can also ensure that specific characteristics of the most profitable customers are measured and understood, so that their needs can continue to be met, but also to support tailored marketing campaigns that will attract the right customers. Finally, measuring customer profitability will often help to highlight ways of improving your relationship with your customers to increase your business value to them. This is important not only as a means of driving more revenue from your customer base, but also as a means of reducing customer defections.

Measuring customer profitability can be achieved by analysing two key issues: customer revenue and customer costs (including defection and retention costs). Some of the most important issues to measure and analyse are detailed in Table 7.1.

Understanding the most and least profitable customers will enable the profit-driven online business to target current and future e-commerce initiatives at the most profitable customers. It will also enable it to find ways of using e-commerce technologies to reduce the costs of doing business with the least profitable customers, while simultaneously helping to increase revenues and profits from that customer group.

Developing a customer's lifetime value to your business

The concept of customer lifetime value is certainly not new, but it is worth considering how customer loyalty, repeat business and increased business develop profitability. First and most obviously, the longer a customer stays with your business, the more they will spend over time. This is profitable because having sold once you are often not having to market or sell to attract them back, you simply need to focus on the quality of your value proposition, rather than your marketing techniques. In addition, this issue of market share can provide a powerful platform from which to develop new commercial opportunities; for example, it can be used to attract advertisers or to entrench your business's position in the market.

Second, customer loyalty and repeat business often lead to referral revenue. If customers are pleased with your service they will tell others, and online they can often be incentivised to do so. Referrals and word of mouth are powerful drivers of online business. The successful 'member get member' initiative of America On-line (AOL) is a high profile example of this.

Third, a satisfied customer can often be receptive to new products, as well as or instead of their original purchase. The key to accomplishing this successfully is, quite simply, to meet their needs through personalisation. By clearly understanding what the customer wants they can be 'up-sold' and 'cross-sold' additional products – and if these new products do not exist, the business can have the confidence to start developing them.

Another benefit of online customer loyalty is the ability to *increase* prices to loyal customers, because, of all the possible purchasers, they are the ones best placed to understand the value of your products. Loyal customers do not typically require discounts or product add-ons to stay with you: if they

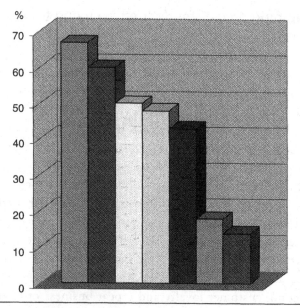

Figure 7.1: Customer needs in the wired world[2]

are happy with the product or service they are buying, and if it is competitive, they will not normally be tempted away.

Finally, market testing of new products is another benefit of customer loyalty; this can not only save money in testing through other means, it is also often much more effective. In addition, it provides an opportunity to develop a loyal customer base for new products, or products that are still in development.

Figure 7.1 shows the findings of a recent limited survey of Internet users and highlights the key priorities for customers using the Internet. Clearly, the ability to deliver on these customer needs is the key to customer loyalty and competitive advantage.

Targeting, attracting and retaining the right customers: the value of mass personalisation

It is said that during the 1950s and 1960s the issue of marketing first came to real prominence for businesses. In the 1970s the focus shifted to mass marketing within an industry, highlighting techniques for reaching customers on a broad scale. In the 1980s and through to the mid-1990s,

> ### KEY CONCEPT
>
> Mass personalisation is the ability to reach individual customers – targeting the right customers and then fulfilling their market needs – on a mass (often global) scale. It is one of the most significant developments in marketing and one of the greatest drivers of revenue and cost savers of the Internet.

the focus moved to market segmentation, improving the way that customers in specific market segments were identified and reached. Now the focus has narrowed even further, with online developments offering businesses the opportunity for mass personalisation, the ability to reach and target individual customers on a mass scale.

 IMPLEMENTATION CHECKLIST: targeting, attracting and retaining the right customers

1   Understand which customers you want to attract and how

It is important to know exactly to whom your product or service will appeal. Once this question has been answered and potential customers have been profiled as closely as possible, the next task is to understand what they want. With this information and insight it is then possible to:

♦ ensure that their needs are met and that your value proposition is compelling and dynamic enough to sustain their interest;

♦ decide how best to appeal to this audience, considering everything from tone of voice to frequency of contact;

♦ decide how to engage this target market: when to ask for their input, whether to offer discounts, and generally how to ensure that the online experience offered by your business is appealing;

♦ decide how to retain and 'capture' or 'hook' enquirers, ensuring that when your site is visited you have the enquirer's details and can follow up later, whether or not they stay and buy.

This list is by no means exhaustive: the key is simply to start focusing on your target market and ways of reaching and attracting them. It is also worth considering two other critical issues. First, not only is it important to understand which customers you want to attract, but also which ones you definitely do not want to lose. Second, It helps to understand that the customer who makes the purchase may not be the key influencer or end-user (for instance, a purchasing department is often not the ultimate customer).

2 Focus on which customers are profitable and measure the key drivers of revenue growth and profitability

This has been mentioned already, but unfortunately businesses often rush headlong into being all things to all people, disregarding the need to retain a focus on the most profitable parts of the market. It is worth remembering that customer loyalty may be important, but if the cost of ensuring a customer's loyalty outweighs the benefits and revenue of that customer, why bother? Maintaining market share for its own sake is often an unwise approach: if a customer cannot be retained or developed (meaning 'upsold' other products) without losing money, then it is better to lose the customer and focus on those who will help improve profitability.

3 Evaluate sources of success and reasons for failure

Chapter 3 discussed the need for a business architecture or structure that dynamically monitors e-commerce developments, maximising successes and pre-empting or swiftly resolving problems. Clearly, this also requires a blame-free, empowered organisational culture to succeed.

4 Understand the dos and don'ts of customer loyalty for the online business

Some of the factors frequently cited as reasons for both success and failure of online activities are listed in Table 7.2.

5 Shift from a product focus to a customer focus, involving customers in your business and moving to mass personalisation

There are several stages in the process of enabling customers to develop a personalised service. The first step is to build trust and rapport with each customer. Listening, understanding and helping are the keys to a successful relationship at any time and the online environment is no exception. The second stage takes this concept a step further, allowing customers to specify and modify the information they give to you, in effect modifying their own profile so that they are telling you what they need. The third stage in the process is

Table 7.2: Achieving success online

Do	Don't
Focus on delivering customers a consistent (and ideally a branded) experience each time they visit your site, order or deal with your business	Over-complicate the site, product offer, strategy or any aspect of the online business. Online, clarity works
Be clear about your value proposition (what you are offering current and potential customers)	Change too frequently . . .
Provide incentives for new customers to return and re-order	. . . or stay the same for too long
Reward loyalty for established customers	Avoid asking the customer or, perhaps more importantly, avoid testing the site from the customer's perspective
Be competitive – what seems like a good deal to you may not be enough to match your competitors in the eyes of your customers	Ignore problems and potential pitfalls: identify them early, resolve them or put contingency plans in place
Make the customer's experience as easy and enjoyable as possible. Ensure that the customer saves time, avoids irritation and is in control	Focus on your internal divisions, products and view of the world; emphasise, instead, issues of greatest relevance and interest to your customers
Reassure customers with a reliable service and product offer that delivers peace of mind	Target everyone – focus on how to appeal to your most profitable customer groups
Continuously improve the process using customer feedback, to enhance customer service and increase profits	Fail to communicate, both internally and externally
Deliver reliability by working with partners and investing where necessary in resources to deliver more to your customers	Control your customers – *they* need to feel in control
Understand that the nature of online business is personal – one customer looking at one screen – and that individuality can be leveraged to benefit your business	Be afraid to question the existing commercial model that may prevail in your industry and don't fail to use the Internet to innovate

to tailor information and special offer promotions to each individual customer profile. The holy grail of marketing has long been the ability to meet the needs of every individual customer to drive revenue and profit, and this is now achievable.

Next, follow through so that the initial purchase is not a once-only transaction but provides an on-going and continuously developing supply of service, information and product offers based on customer needs. Other factors are also recognised as being of value and often their value and relevance depends on the type of market, product and customer as well as the competitive situation. Two other issues need to be considered when moving to a customer focus and delivering mass personalisation. The first is the need to be as open and transparent in your business activities as possible. This can mean communicating and informing customers in a helpful way, but one that also lets them feel that they have a stake in your success (as indeed they do!). The second is the idea of fostering community, so that customers leave behind on your web site something of value to other customers. This can enhance the value of the site for everyone concerned, but it also encourages customers to get involved and hence feel a sense of ownership, as well as having a reason to return. It also helps to make the site unique.

Building an online brand

What your online business activities should strive to achieve is a loyal and supportive base of customers who want your products and want them from you. The online environment is particularly useful in this regard as it is flexible, offering scope for personalisation and the means to build a distinctive value proposition. If this is compelling and attractive to customers, the result is a strong online identity, a powerful brand that can be nurtured and developed to create new opportunities, to increase market share, to increase shareholder value or simply to benefit customers and drive profits. Loyal customers and strong brands are best viewed together, as two sides of the same coin. If one is reduced the other is too; if one is strengthened both elements are stronger.

It is also useful to consider that brands have their own personalities: they change and develop, but they also leave an impression on customers. Managing a brand's (a product's or a business's) *personality* online is demanding. The Internet can provide greater opportunity and flexibility if used effectively, but it can also damage a brand and alienate customers if several critical factors are overlooked. One critical issue to watch is the fact that brand personalities, perceptions and customers' trust require time to build – and the one commodity that is often not available online is time. Even so, developing small 'wins' in the eyes of the customer, coupled with a clear understanding of the principles guiding the development of the brand, will enable it to strengthen.

The advantages of brands in the online environment

Brand management and positioning are key factors influencing strategy and sustained business profitability for online businesses. They link closely with other issues such as competitive strategy, pricing, segmentation and market-entry strategies.

Brands can be seen as key intangible resources (as distinct from tangible ones of cash, customers, premises). As an intangible resource, a brand needs to be carefully developed and maintained. Its features may include, for example, reputation, loyalty and understanding among customers, and these factors need actively to inform decisions affecting the brand.

Brands can also be leveraged: for example, a market leader can diversify or strengthen its pre-eminence through the launch of a brand for the online environment. An example of this is the development of FT.com and Economist.com as separate brands in their own right, distinguishing themselves from their parent brands chiefly in their dynamic, customer-centric approach. They are given a head start and considerable advantage through their link with the main brand. Finally, central to the issue of profitably managing a brand is the need for that brand to be clearly and consistently positioned in the market. Again, this needs constant development to ensure that the brand remains dynamic and holds its place relative to its competitors.

Brand personality

Brands are hugely complex and varied assets and, much like people, they possess specific distinguishing features. The concept of brand personality highlights the power of brands and provides a wealth of valuable intangible resources such as goodwill, loyalty and respect.

How brands can develop profitability online

The advantages of brands as a driver of profitability online include pricing benefits. A successful and established brand can often command a substantial price premium, exceeding the extra cost in terms of production and marketing. Reinforcing the product's appeal is particularly important in the online environment where customers may not know whom to trust or what they are likely to receive from the online vendor. Another way in which brands drive profitability online is their ability to foster customer loyalty, as key customer groups can identify preferred brands easily, becoming repeat purchasers. Using brand extension, businesses can effectively launch profitable new products online by exploiting the popularity and strength of an established brand. Brands also offer the opportunity to enter new markets: a strong brand can enable the product to cascade from one market into another, thereby spreading in popularity.

Case Study: Financial Times

FT Knowledge is an example of this approach, where the strong and established *Financial Times* (FT) brand – probably one of the UK's strongest – was developed to launch a new business, providing business education and management development. This in turn can provide a feedback loop, reinforcing the brand still further by attacking the competition, adding another dimension to the brand (innovation) and developing new markets (the online training market). The benefits here are twofold: a strong brand often makes it easier to introduce new products by exploiting 'brand equity', and opportunities are created by branding to open up new market segments.

Another advantage of brands online is that they can extend the life of a product. By their nature, brands combine trust, respect, profile and marketing spend, and this can often be co-ordinated to inject new life into a declining product, *even a whole industry*. Finally, brands provide a valuable, market-oriented focus for online businesses to structure themselves, enabling enterprises to organise themselves around the marketing of the product.

Techniques for building an online brand

1 Establishing trust

The first element in brand building online is the need to establish trust. Transferring, or partnering with, a well-known offline brand can quickly achieve this. However, the process of leveraging real-world brand

KEY CONCEPT

It is important to appreciate from the outset that goodwill and trust, the real advantages to a business and its customers of a strong brand, take time and a history of reliable activity to develop.

equity only works if the offline brand is strong, appealing and commensurate with the online product; above all, it needs to engender the customer's trust. If this is not possible or desirable, the solution is to work hard at building trust: simplicity, ease, reliability and customer focus all help, but perhaps the single most effective method of achieving trust is through communication – and the Internet certainly facilitates that. If the brand is new – perhaps resulting from a new product launch, or possibly even the launch of a new online business – it is worth spending time to map out the brand values that you want to associate with your business. Ideally, these should reflect the character and needs of the target market.

Once these have been decided, the next stage is to implement them in all aspects of the online brand, from the layout of the home page to the tone of voice in the copy and the content itself. In fact, the ten critical drivers of e-business success will determine the appeal and personality of a brand. (To recap, these drivers are content, communication, customer care, community and culture, convenience and ease, connectivity, cost and profitability, customisation, capability and competitiveness.)

2 Market segmentation

Market segmentation is another key element in building an effective brand and it is of enormous significance on the Internet. Many web sites seem to believe that they need to appeal to the whole world, when in fact a clear focus on their target audience would go a long way to building their appeal. For the online brand to succeed, the web site – and everything to do with it – needs to reflect the nature and needs of the target group.

3 Communication

Communication (what is said to the *customer* and how, as well as how the *business reacts* to what it is told) is also highly relevant to brand building online. To establish a successful brand, communication on the web site must first generate an immediate interest in a product or service. One method of achieving this is to create a link between the product and a particular need or motivation within the target group, which often requires an understanding of the target group's psychographic profile (a combination of demographic features and behavioural preferences). The second aim of communication from the web site must be to create awareness and a favourable impression of the brand and product. The key to achieving this online is for the web site to hold the customer's interest in the first 20–30 seconds; if this is not achieved, it is likely that the customer will leave the site.

Creating an intention to buy is the next aim of communication on the web site. For those products where the customer is looking to buy and has a favourable impression of the brand, the site needs to present the product and facilitate its purchase. Once the intention to buy has been established, the final communication aim of the site must be to effect the purchase, enabling customers either to buy online conveniently and easily, or else directing them to a distributor or place where they can buy. If the latter approach is chosen, there may need to be an incentive to follow the process through from the online to the offline world.

 IMPLEMENTATION CHECKLIST: ideas and issues to address when building a brand online

The following closely related issues are some of the key areas to consider before establishing a brand online.

Brand purpose

1   How can the brand best be used online? For example, is it to raise profile, provide reassurance or create an intention to buy?

2   What benefits can the brand offer customers? These benefits may be either emotional or rational.

3   How reliable and trustworthy is the brand? Is it credible in the eyes of the customer?

4   What is the market value of the brand – is it increasing or declining, and what affects its success?

Brand personality

5   What are the brand values? What are its qualities (how can these best be described)?

6   How does the brand look and feel and to whom does it appeal?

7   What tone of voice does the brand have online? Is this commensurate with the brand values, target market and any existing perceptions?

Brand competitiveness

8   How does the brand differentiate the product or business from its competitors?

9   How unique is the brand and how easy would it be to replicate? (Ideally, there should be sufficient barriers to replication to ensure that the brand remains strong and unique.)

10   What are the strengths and weaknesses of the brand?

11   How strong and credible is the brand in the eyes of the customer?

12   Can the brand be stretched into new markets? If so, how far, in what direction and what are the values that enable

(or could enable) this? If not, it may be that the brand is too narrowly focused or weak.

13 Is there sufficient investment in all aspects of the brand? How can it be strengthened and enhanced?

Using the Internet for profitable product innovation

CHAPTER 8

Overview

New product development can be fast or slow, reactive, adaptive or proactive – but it is almost always hazardous. In addition, existing products can often get left behind; in some businesses this was true even before the arrival of the new economy, but now with the pace of change and development moving at previously unimagined speeds, it is particularly significant. The Internet can provide existing products with a new lease of life if they are already successful and a second chance to get it right if they were less than perfect initially.

Some of the key issues to consider are ways in which the online business can add value to existing (or historical) products; develop product extensions; repackage and repurpose products and services; and

---

CONTINUED . . . Overview

relaunch existing products and services. This chapter
will examine techniques for profitable product development, including:

- innovation using the Internet;
- understanding product positioning;
- protecting intellectual property rights.

Innovation using the Internet

How the Internet will help companies innovate

In Chapter 2 we outlined the ten critical drivers of online
success, most of which rely on innovation for their success.
Of course the relationship is symbiotic, with the innovation
online springing most readily from the ten critical drivers. As
recent research summarised in Table 8.1 highlights, content,
communication, customer care, convenience and ease,
customisation, cost control, capability (dynamic, responsive
and flexible) and competitiveness all rely on an innovative
approach, in particular an ability creatively to develop new
products and services online.

Table 8.1: How the Internet will help companies innovate

	% of respondents
Create new Internet-based products or services	60
Enable innovative knowledge to be disseminated	59
Provide closer ties to innovative suppliers/partners	58
Improve communication throughout product development	55
Enable increased product customisation	40

Source: EIU and Booz Allen & Hamilton[2]

Case Study: Building an innovative online business – Construction Plus

An interesting example of successful business innovation is the case of Construction Plus, launched by Emap Digital in 2000, which has rapidly become one of the most visited industry web sites in Europe. Essentially, the site enables the construction industry – from architects to builders to lawyers – to access online information and business tools. It contains a massive amount of information, including a database of companies supplying over 150 000 construction and related products, 80 construction news stories each day, a rolling total of around 800 industry job vacancies, and sales leads from more than 30 000 construction projects. Of course, this would all count for little if the site were not successful. The *month after it launched* it received over 450 000 page impressions, and this had reached 800 000 impressions a month within seven months of launch.

Emap, an established offline publisher, avoided the traps of many other traditional publishers when launching this venture. Rather than simply putting existing material on the Web, it understood the need to use the *medium* of the web, choosing to focus on the key drivers of e-commerce success, notably content, community and capability. The success of Construction Plus in such a short time can be attributed to the following:

- *A well-designed site* that is easy to use and understand, yet also able consistently to deliver comprehensive, appropriate and interesting content for its target audience.
- *A dynamic approach* that realises the need constantly to refresh and renew its offering.

CONTINUED . . . Case Study: Building an innovative online business – Construction Plus

- *A commercial approach* that gained the support of 30 influential construction companies as launch partners. In this way, the site not only generated a valuable revenue stream but enhanced its credibility from the start, improving the value it could offer its customers and the sense of community among all of its stakeholders.

- *An understanding of the importance of communication and community.* In common with most industries, construction relies heavily and increasingly on effective networking among players in the industry. The site facilitates communication among businesses involved in construction so that it not only provides information, but does so in a way that improves business processes and adds real value for customers. For example, the site is built around a series of portals focusing on distinct communities such as architects, as well as setting up partnerships with leading building merchants.

Customisation and customer-intelligent products and services

One of the main challenges facing companies is to drive success by providing personalised products and services, while simultaneously reducing costs. As the need to drive competitive advantage narrows the distinctions between companies offering similar personalised products, companies need to innovate and challenge the accepted norms in order to emerge as the industry leader.

Products tailored to individual preferences and capable of continuously adapting to changing needs may once have seemed fanciful or far-fetched, but online they are both a reality and a powerful source of competitive advantage. Increasingly, products that are continuously customised in response to customer needs and preferences are being developed and valued by customers.

> **KEY CONCEPT**
>
> It is no longer enough to offer one-off, limited customisation. By leveraging all the information, expertise and new technology available, companies must tailor products and services to adapt to a customer's *changing* requirements.

This concept is known as *customer-intelligent value* and it greatly enhances the value of the product. Achieving this is not easy: efficient personalisation requires businesses to build the potential to respond to changing needs and new technologies into the product or service.

Advantages of developing customer-intelligent value

At the outset, it is important to understand the advantages of developing customer-intelligent value online, as these can be significant. The aim is to develop the ability increasingly to match customers' individual needs and wants, over time; if successful, this can provide powerful competitive advantages. Developing customer-intelligent value enables your business to:

- *Stay close to the customer* – for many years a common call of management experts, and perhaps the most common dictum for business success, has been 'stay as close to the customer as possible'. Customer-intelligent value offers the best opportunity yet to integrate the customer into the firm's business system. The Internet enables businesses to build strong relationships with their individual customers, and these relationships are beginning to extend beyond the specific exchanges required to customise the product.

Involving the customer in the design and realization of the product creates value and only by more and more deeply involving customers can the company learn and respond effectively. This happens when the involvement is at the very general level required for process improvement, as well as the individual level.

- *Create sales opportunities that are genuinely valued by the customer* – in contrast to the policy of planned obsolescence employed by some businesses, customer-intelligent value can create products that can be upgraded, enhanced and even fundamentally altered without replacing the product itself.

- *Use information so precisely that little money, energy, time or other resources are wasted* – increasingly, companies are facing the dual challenge of being a low-cost operator in their industries and also the most customer responsive. Moving beyond mass customisation – where products are partly standardised (80–90 per cent) and partly customised (10–20 per cent) – to meet the differentiated needs of customers on a one-to-one basis requires companies to sense, respond and adapt their products to the individual experience of each customer.

Vital questions and answers

. . . when preparing for profitable product development online

1 Understand the market, in particular, the needs of customers and how these can be met more efficiently using the Internet

The first stage is to understand the market as clearly and closely as possible. This may involve market research, and the priorities need to be:

CONTINUED . . . **Vital questions and answers**

- *defining customers' needs* and understanding which features of the product will be most appealing;
- *targeting the product* and determining, in as great a level of detail as possible, who the product will appeal to and who will buy;
- *understanding market trends* affecting a range of issues including pricing, market expectations (and history, where relevant) and technological developments.

2 Learn from experience (yours and others')

Understand how and why other products have failed or succeeded and define the product's critical success factors. What is it that will enable the product to succeed? What are the issues that will drive and deliver success? Where are the pitfalls?

3 Consider competitors

Understand who the main competitors are, now and in the future. This means assessing:

- competitors' strengths and weaknesses;
- their likely and potential responses to your new product;
- how your product can gain *and sustain* market share from competitors.

4 Consider the overall product portfolio

This requires an assessment of how the new product fits with current products and others in development. In particular, two questions are significant:

CONTINUED ... **Vital questions and answers**

- Does it complement the full product portfolio, offering a complementary (rather than competitive or disjointed) range of products? (Building a product portfolio is like assembling a winning football team – no one wants 11 goalkeepers!)
- How well does it support the overall strategy of the business?

5 Consider other markets – are there lessons to learn?

Different strategies and innovations can come from experience, creative genius or, quite often, adapting the work and ideas of others. To do this, it is often worth considering how similar issues, ranging from market research to developing customer loyalty, have been addressed in other markets and industries. This may start a process leading to a totally new approach and it may result in a fresh competitive advantage.

6 Focus on the product's benefits and commercial marketing issues

When developing the product or planning and designing the service, it is vital to keep in mind the key market issues, including:

- What will make it unique?
- What features will be used to sell the product?
- How will the product be sold?
- Where will the product be sold (and by whom)?
- What will be the pricing strategy?
- What sales volumes can be expected?

CONTINUED . . . **Vital questions and answers**

7 Focus on production and product profitability

Internal processes, notably production, are as fundamental to profitability as are external market issues. There
are many different issues to review here, including:

- Are the processes, skills and resources in place to
  produce the product?
- Is production financially viable?
- How liable to change are costs?
- How reliable are suppliers?
- How can quality be ensured?
- How much will it cost to develop?
- Can production meet anticipated demand? How will
  fluctuations in demand be handled?

8 Consider the main financial issues

These clearly need to be considered at every stage of the
development process. Specific issues include the *amount* of
investment required, the *timing* and the *level of risk*
involved. Consider how much investment is required;
whether there are other priorities for investment, and
how significant is the commercial risk in developing the
product (as well as not developing it).

9 Focus on people

Staffing and skill levels are often decisive in the product
development process. Fundamental issues to consider
include:

- Are there skilled staff in place to develop, market and
  distribute the product?

CONTINUED ... Vital questions and answers

- Where do the skills gaps lie within the organisation (and the development process) and what can be done to bridge them?

Profit-driven innovation in the online business

There are many ways to develop new products or boost the profitability of existing ones using the Internet. For some businesses this process comes easily: it may start with an energetic and visionary entrepreneur, or it may happen by accident (if only very occasionally). However, there are several fundamental principles for online innovation that will help to drive the process and ensure that it remains customer and profit focused (see Table 8.2).

The value of product positioning

The concept of positioning relates to how a product is perceived by customers *relative to its competitors*. It originated in the advertising industry as a way of identifying what attributes of the product should be imbedded in the buyer's consciousness: for example, it may be cheap, innovative, cool, high quality or something else. Positioning helps to support a strategic focus that will lead to success. It is essentially about influencing attitudes and perceptions about a product or company brand, rather than changing the product itself. Positioning is useful for improving performance by increasing awareness of a company's or product's capabilities, refreshing or reinforcing an existing brand and explaining a specific concept.

Table 8.2: Principles for online innovation

Technique	Making it work for the online business
Understand the market and the customers' priorities and current situation	• Research customers' views – request information, provide incentives for the customer to speak to you and help you shape your product offer • Research competitors – in the same industry and in other industries, understanding different business models and critical success factors • Meet with customers and get them to understand your business and 'give of themselves'. It is never too early to start building trust and loyalty online • Consider how you would solve your customers' problems
Brainstorm	• The pace of business online changes so far and so fast that regularly looking for new ideas and ways of improving business operations is sensible. This may be achieved by changing perspective, perhaps swapping roles, putting yourself in the customer's position, or looking at other businesses and industries facing similar issues • Brainstorming can also occur under pressure, perhaps as part of a problem-solving process, or it may take place on an *ad hoc* basis, in response to a particular issue, idea or situation. This needs to be done in a positive, open environment, usually with new ideas measured against strict criteria • Asking people at all levels in the organisation, including customers and suppliers as well as staff, can also be invaluable for generating creative new ideas
Hire and retain talented people with ideas and energy (and experience too!)	A premium is often placed on people with experience of doing things a particular way. However, what often matters more is a 'can do' approach combined with an understanding of what is possible and what is important. Adopting a more flexible, imaginative approach to recruiting and retaining talented staff is often what counts most. Consider how to incentivise people to generate ideas and to implement them effectively
Ensure that the business is *focused* on innovation	There are few things as debilitating or frustrating as a constant raft of initiatives lacking in priority, resources or leadership. Often this can appear as if the business, which may be doing well, is dissatisfied with the current state of play. There is a lot to be said for the old adage, 'if it ain't broke, don't fix it'. (I prefer the slightly newer adage, 'if it's utterly and completely broken, don't fix it either'. A brand new approach may be needed, not a bandage. This saying, of course, originated from Winnie-the-Pooh by A. A. Milne.) Delivering focus in the online business can be accomplished by: • Establishing a clear process for new developments • Putting key staff in charge of driving innovation and improvements

Table 8.2: (continued)

Technique	Making it work for the online business
	• Facilitating knowledge sharing, normally using IT systems and efficient organisation structures • Ensuring that best-practice expertise is shared • Inviting and acting on customer suggestions
Review and streamline business processes	Understanding what works (best practice), what customers want and what needs to be delivered is one thing, but this understanding can count for nothing if it is not effectively *implemented*. Innovation therefore needs to go the whole way, from initial idea to delivering customer value. As well as using the techniques mentioned above, this can be achieved by reviewing existing processes and activities from the customer's viewpoint and asking how greater profitability can be achieved?

 GETTING STARTED: essential techniques for product positioning

The following techniques are useful to achieve distinction or to stake a claim effectively in a specific market segment.

1 Understand the market

This means finding a niche or part of the market where there is space to establish and maintain a profitable position. This requires an understanding of not only the market, but the key trends and factors that are influencing it. This may demand the recognition that in certain markets at certain times there are no attainable positions left.

2 Focus on the customer

When planning or considering the position of the product or business, it is important to remain externally focused and consider how the customer will perceive and react to the message or offer. Or, to put it another way, what message will have the greatest impact on the customer in the way that is intended?

3 Timing is important

Positioning is often easiest when you are the first into a new market: the 'first-mover advantage'. From this position it is possible to get to know the customer and market in detail and build a strong customer base, even a rapport with customers. Invariably the brand image is an attractive one of responsiveness and innovation. For brands that are not the first mover, it is important to choose the right moment to launch, ideally when the market leader is weak or quiet, or both.

4 Avoid head-on confrontation with the market leader

The brand with the most to lose is the market leader, which will therefore react very powerfully against newcomers and use all its available resources. Key among these resources are the very ones that make it market leader, usually wealth, fame and hordes of customers. The brand that is attacking the market leader therefore needs some valuable, attention-grabbing distinguishing feature, and the ability to convey this strongly in its message.

5 Consistency is essential and positioning means striving for leadership in a particular area

Once a position has been taken, it needs to be consistently and unfailingly defended. More than that, it needs to be actively developed or the potential benefits of occupying that position will erode, crumble or fade.

> **KEY CONCEPT**
>
> Success lies with the business whose message and offer – its value proposition – is focused on the customer in a way that is clear, straightforward and powerfully communicated.

6 Choose a powerful and simple message

To be fully effective the message needs to be clear, simple and consistent. Online the tendency all too often is to overcomplicate.

Market entry: choosing a market position for your online business

There are generally perceived to be three market-entry positions for any business:

- first mover (or pioneer);
- early adopter (or second/third mover);
- follower.

First movers

There are significant implications for the online business in each of these market positions. Clearly, the first mover can define the product offer, setting standards and, most valuably, gaining market share and brand awareness. However, the difficulties of being a first mover or pioneer are significant: they include the danger of spending too much time and energy building market share and the likelihood that technological developments will be too consuming, either distracting the business leaders or constraining them. The lack of best practice is a weakness: there are often no lessons for the first mover to learn, and no empirical knowledge of where the pitfalls lie.

There are no easy solutions to these issues, but the first movers that have managed to succeed (such as Dell, eBay and Amazon.com) have all demonstrated several features. These are the importance of listening to their customers; building and entrenching market share *swiftly*, and constantly driving innovations so that there is a stream of new products entering the market, ensuring that they do not get left behind or become perceived as yesterday's company.

Early adopters

The early adopter can benefit from the luxury of choosing two possible approaches to developing its business: either selecting the most profitable or promising market segments or product niches, or choosing the basic offering but adding additional features that will defeat the first mover. The advantage is clearly that the early adopter can learn from the first mover's mistakes – or success – and ensure that its approach takes this to the next level as far as the customer is concerned. The problems for the early adopter are that it will, inevitably, be compared to the first mover; every aspect of its offer and its relative strengths and weaknesses will be scrutinised, a situation avoided by the first mover. Also, the early adopter needs to attack an entrenched market position and attract customers who may well be perfectly pleased and loyal with their 'first love', the first mover. As if that were not enough, the margins are unlikely to be the same for the early adopter, as new market entrants usually result in price pressures and a squeeze on margins.

The solutions to these issues again come from a clear focus on markets, customers and profits. The obvious approach is to target those areas where the first mover is weak – either structurally or in the eyes of the market – or where it is not being responsive to the market. The second approach is clearly to differentiate the early adopter from the first mover, perhaps by delivering a message that attacks the market leader or emphasises a vital source of competitive advantage. The early adopter needs to know its strengths and its sources of competitive advantage – not only against the first mover but against other potential market entrants – and emphasise these factors. Early adopters can often succeed by focusing on *improving quality* and *reducing prices*, both of which start with an understanding of customers but are frequently delivered by establishing efficient processes, value chains and supplier relations. This is also important when fighting the (almost) inevitable price war.

Followers

This group has the luxury of having the clearest view of the market, able to focus on analysing trends, best practices and business opportunities. The problems here are the most significant, obvious and hardest to overcome; there is often a herd of followers stampeding into a market (if there is not, that is at least as worrying!) and the difficulty is finding a sufficiently distinctive product offering. The most effective approach is to focus on meeting the needs of specific, tightly defined market segments and not deviating from that market. Also important is the need to exploit cost advantages or economies of scale: this can be done by growing the business out of an existing business, effectively leveraging and building current resources.

It is worth mentioning that once the market has been entered the business becomes the incumbent, a position requiring sustained market focus, innovation and a capacity to constantly develop sources of competitive advantage (these priorities are discussed further in Chapter 12, Resource building: the key to the competitive online business). The best approach clearly depends on a range of factors, but most significant are the nature of the business, the culture of the organisation and the competitiveness of the market.

Managing the potential for channel conflict

Channel conflict affects those businesses that sell via a range of different channels, such as online and via distributors or retail outlets. Problems and conflicts can arise suddenly, without anyone necessarily being aware of any problems or difficulties until it is too late. It is, therefore, worth the profit-driven online business considering its respective channels in detail, as part of the process of product development and innovation. Strength and flexibility are the main areas on which to focus and key issues to consider include the following:

- Assessing the relative value, significance and potential of each separate channel. Clearly, those channels that are most profitable now need to be maintained, but it is also vital to assess the potential relevance of other, smaller channels; for established offline businesses this may include the Internet.
- Understanding the competitiveness of each channel: where are you most vulnerable, now and in the future, and what is being done to address these weaknesses?
- Ensuring that each channel has a slightly different value proposition, one that emphasises the advantages of that specific channel. This may require different, targeted sales and marketing programmes that are clearly focused on the needs of each specific market segment.
- Understanding the customers' perceptions of the brand in general and each product in particular, and knowing where your product is in the market (e.g. number one, top ten or virtually unnoticed) and where it is heading in the mind of the customer (e.g. improving, declining or useless!).
- Delivering the strong leadership needed to act boldly, swiftly and decisively and seeing through these decisions to their conclusion.
- Building on past and current successes to establish a successful and profitable future for the business.

Protecting intellectual property rights

Intellectual property rights (IPR) are an important part of business innovation online; they are also a difficult, complex and

> ### KEY CONCEPT
>
> It is important that once an innovation is developed it is protected. Intellectual property rights have enormous value, delivering vital sources of competitive advantage. The pace of change online unfortunately means that many businesses do not try to protect their intellectual property, which can be expensive to develop. In the long term, the costs of this approach can be high.

specialised area of activity. However, property rights are an important source of value for the profit-driven online business. The key issues to consider – and on which to seek specialist guidance and advice – include patents, which provide protection for unique technical innovations, notably products and manufacturing processes that are better than their predecessors. Designs are also a form of IPR and give protection to the appearance of manufactured products, while trademarks protect brand names and commercial labels that distinguish products, which can have a significant market value. Copyright protection relates to artistic works (usually musical or literary); this is also important for online businesses in the areas of broadcast media and software. In this important, fast-developing and complex area, the best source of advice in my experience is a specialist lawyer who is an expert in the management and protection of IPR. It is also worth remembering that this issue, together with the related legal issues of online security, are among the fastest changing issues on the Internet.

Suppliers and supply chains: reducing costs and adding value

CHAPTER 9

Overview

Whole industries – from automotive manufacturing to retailing – are being revolutionised by technology-driven changes affecting suppliers and supply chains. These developments can either increase costs and result in failure, or they can reduce costs, improve service and dramatically improve competitiveness and overall profitability. Furthermore, managing suppliers of technology to create and drive the success of the profit-driven e-business, is notoriously fraught with potential problems and difficulties.

This chapter will:

- Analyse the key determinants of success for online supplier management.
- Outline practical ways in which the profit-driven e-business can reduce costs and enhance profits through its suppliers and systems.

Techniques for profitable online supplier management

The importance of supplier management for cost reduction

If purchases from suppliers are where costs lie, this is where the greatest attention should be placed to achieve significant cost reductions. Many companies have virtually no information regarding the root causes of the costs and prices they experience from their vendors, and it is this ability to manage, control and use information in partnership with suppliers that makes the online environment so important. To understand the relative importance of purchased materials, it is useful to consider that for many

> **KEY CONCEPT**
>
> In the online environment it is feasible for businesses to streamline their development and delivery processes, frequently providing a better and more competitive customer service. Managing information, suppliers and business processes using information systems is one of the main opportunities and challenges for e-businesses.

businesses (particularly in manufacturing industry) purchases from vendors may represent 50 per cent or more of every dollar of revenue. Investments in managing suppliers and supply chains are therefore critical.

In addition to managing the cost of purchases, online supplier management frequently enables businesses to add value for the customer during the production process, with the emphasis being on where in the value chain the business can derive additional benefit, either by reducing cost or improving the product or service. If other businesses can take care of a particular aspect of the supply chain better than the core business, they should be allowed to do so. This not only reduces costs but increases focus on the core business, allowing the business to deliver the best overall service to the customer. Analysing the supply chain leading to the customer is a valuable method of reducing cost and enhancing competitiveness.

Techniques for cost-effective supplier management

Managing information to ensure cost reduction

Information management is important in the whole area of purchasing and vendor cost management and reduction. One needs to know what one buys, in what quantities, from what vendors. It is also vitally important to be aware of common or potentially common purchases across businesses, as well as information regarding vendor performance. Customer information as well as internally analysed business data can be leveraged to deliver greater productivity, profitability and customer focus.

Standardising specifications and working closely with suppliers

For any business there is a wide range of drivers of high material costs, many internally generated. For example, if every new product development project starts without the benefit of previous experience and knowledge and produces a unique set of specifications, many unnecessary costs will be incurred that could have been avoided by ensuring standardisation. For the e-business, costs can be reduced and product specifications can often be standardised in the following ways:

- Assessing customer preferences for existing online product purchases.
- Researching customer preferences for new products and product extensions on the web site, possibly piloting different options.

- Reviewing the value chain (the range of business processes that result in the final product being delivered to the customer) to assess where others can add greater value and where costs can be reduced – leading to outsourcing of certain activities.

To achieve these benefits it is often desirable to work closely with suppliers, sharing details of plans, aims and customer knowledge. If vendors' costs can be reduced by 10–20 per cent and the customer could be expected to share in half of that, and materials represent 50 per cent or more of a customer's costs, such a reduction could have a significant impact on the customer's cost or the business's profit structure. Opportunities that can have long-term benefits for both parties include:

- application of activity-based costing to determine product costs and cost drivers;
- utilisation of process analysis and mapping to identify and eliminate waste;
- rearrangement of facilities;
- set-up time reduction;
- application of target costing at the vendor level.

Value chain analysis

Businesses may be thought of as a series of major processes, sub-processes and activities. At the major processes level one might think in terms of market assessment, new product development, outside procurement, inside operations, distribution, sales and service. Such a sequence has been referred to as the 'value chain'. The chain is obvious; the term 'value' is intended to indicate where along the chain value is created, or potentially dissipated. In the last few years the argument has been put forward that a firm should concentrate on its core competencies and capabilities, and that it should outsource those processes that are not core to its success and could be performed more proficiently by others.

Some businesses selling to other businesses (B2B) think in terms of extended value chains, analysing upstream the capabilities and performance of suppliers and their suppliers, and downstream customers and their customers. Being able to make such analyses and deciding on appropriate courses of action require different information, in many cases not readily found within the firm's own accounting records or in a typical understanding of related parties' activities.

Reducing the costs of the purchasing process

In addition to standardising specifications and rationalising the number and scope of suppliers, there is frequently the opportunity to take costs out of the procurement process itself. Traditionally, many paper forms have been associated with placing orders, expediting, receiving, storing, accounting and paying vendors. Some companies have dramatically reduced or virtually eliminated such costs. E-commerce, blanket purchase orders, vendors on site and payment on the basis of customer usage of vendor materials are some of the ways in which such administrative costs have been reduced.

Outsourcing

One approach that has often been deployed in the past few years is the idea of outsourcing a firm's activities to a third party (frequently a consultancy). This may be applied to service functions such as finance and technology systems management. Many companies have found that the high technology and rapid change involved with their IT activities have been such that it is difficult for line managers to stay up to date: communication between IT functions and managers has become strained and budgets have grown into black holes. In an effort to focus on what they do best and 'unbundle' much of the rest, a number of large corporations have outsourced most of their information systems and technology activities.

Where and how a firm spends and makes money, and how that may be measured and improved, requires information to be cut in new and different ways. It is necessary to think and use cost information in a value chain orientation rather than according to functions and cost centres. Understanding costs and benefits, and considering costs differently depending on the specific decision to be made, is not easy. It requires a good information foundation and the ability to utilise that information intelligently.

Case Study: Using the Internet to reconfigure the supply chain – Gateway

Gateway established itself in a pre-eminent, but difficult to sustain, position as the first manufacturer in the world to sell PCs online. Keeping up this eye-catching and market-leading position led Gateway to place the Web at the centre of its business. In particular, this has meant implementing a streamlined supply chain management process that aims to deliver PCs built to order (with no stock of finished items or high inventory costs reducing margins) within eight working days of an order being placed. Key features of the Gateway supply chain management system include:

- *An efficient ordering process*, including a web order entry system operating in each of its retail outlets, and an advanced intelligent e-commerce 'configurator' on its web site so that, using a drop-down menu system, customers can specify the type of system they require, trying out different modifications before they buy and monitoring the price of the system they are designing.
- *A system that is reliable from start to finish*. Given the nature of the business, it is important that the supply

---

CONTINUED . . . Case Study: Using the Internet to reconfigure the supply chain – Gateway

chain process is customer focused, meaning that it needs to be easy to understand, simple to use, swift, flexible and reliable – it must work consistently.

- *Partnerships* with different organisations to provide their customers with peripherals and accessories, product delivery and software products.

It is often rightly said that without customers and without cash there would not be a successful business, but it is equally true that without an efficient supply chain management system to deliver profitably what the customer wants, the business would suffer and die. The keys to Gateway's success include innovation and a realisation that the business must develop new ways of working to maintain their profile and profitability. More than ever, successful e-businesses understand that no matter how illustrious their past, they are only as good as their next three months' order book, and supply chain management often provides a valuable source of competitive advantage online.

Reducing costs and boosting profits with supplier management

 IMPLEMENTATION CHECKLIST: four key stages of effective supplier and systems management

Implementing new software systems, adding new suppliers and altering the supply chain process have common issues and stages for the e-business. Each of the four stages is explained in detail in the following pages:

1 Agreeing the business aims and required architecture (meaning the organisational structure) to ensure a profitable, customer-focused supply chain.
2 Evaluating and selecting suppliers and applications to ensure that they are linked into the business, sharing the same objectives and knowledge as the e-business.
3 Ensuring the success of the supplier management process.
4 Monitoring progress and continuously refining and enhancing the supply chain process to benefit the customer and deliver greater progress.

1 Agreeing the business aims and establishing the organisational architecture

From the outset, the vision and strategy for the profit-driven e-business need to be clearly defined, and this requires active and sustained senior management commitment and involvement. Specifically, senior managers must:

◆ *Set the vision* – monitoring competitors, understanding customer preferences, monitoring shifting market conditions and evaluating internal cost structures are all decisive factors influencing the vision and aims of the e-business. A clear direction needs to be set and 'sold' so that employees understand it; the direction should also be reflected in all aspects of the business, including the supply chain.
◆ *Match the vision to the e-commerce architecture* – senior managers need to understand what the vision means for the organisation of their e-business activities. For example, if the business is a traditional publishing company providing financial information in paper format,

it might decide that it needs to reconstruct itself to match (or lead) its markets, which require information in electronic format online. This move to become an e-business is clearly central to the publisher's success; in the future, the majority of its revenues may come from online activities. In these circumstances, the business needs to evaluate and consider changing its business processes; marketing, sales and distribution methods; suppliers, and the skill sets of its employees. This highlights the fact that developing a profit-driven e-business is a major change process and needs to be recognised as such. The example is relevant to a traditional business transforming itself into an e-business: what is vital is that senior managers recognise their organisation's position on a scale of e-business development, which almost always relates to the business's historical development and the prevailing market trends.

◆ *Establish performance standards and drive compliance with those standards* – while it is not necessary for senior managers to decide exactly what technology is adopted, it is important that they set specific performance standards that are customer focused. These should enable the business to compete and deliver in such areas as price, service quality, delivery times, flexibility and customisation. However, in addition the organisation must recognise that a successful e-business is not static and that in the online environment customer expectations and industry standards are constantly evolving and improving.

◆ *Ensure that the organisation structure is both robust and flexible, enabling the business both to grow and to respond effectively to problems* – one of the critical issues relating to e-business structure is the ability to react swiftly and decisively to problems. Organisations must monitor e-business demand very carefully, as the risks are that either they will develop an expensive operation without customer demand that struggles to be profitable, or demand outstrips the ability of the e-business to respond and meet customers' expectations. As well as forecasting demand and adjusting their resources to match, the business needs to ensure that there are adequate contingency plans in place to cope with network problems and interruptions that may affect the quality of service to customers, ultimately affecting customer loyalty.

2   Evaluating and selecting suppliers and applications to ensure that they are linked into the business

◆ *Evaluating and selecting suppliers* – choosing the right e-commerce supplier is important to success, not only because the costs are significant but also because many other issues – ranging from competitiveness to risk – are affected by the final choice of supplier. Effective techniques to consider when evaluating and managing suppliers are:

- *Create a team to initiate and lead the process* – this needs to be an interdisciplinary team, ideally one that was involved in formulating the e-business strategy. This broad scope of expertise, continuity and under-standing of the business is often decisive in ensuring success.

- *Agree on the specific objectives that the supplier will be required to achieve* – the first action for the team should be to set business objectives that are specific, measurable, achievable, realistic and time focused, which the supplier and technology are intended to meet. Once these objectives are set, an invitation to tender is often the next step, with the objectives and general requirements of the business outlined so that the vendor has enough information to provide a realistic, detailed and consistent proposal, but is also able to innovate and suggest new, value-adding approaches. This invitation to tender can be sent to a range of suppliers, and it may be wise to select six or so potential suppliers, with a mix of well-known and well-established companies often combined with start-ups and smaller organisations.

- *Develop and apply criteria to test how effectively each supplier meets the required criteria* – it is important that each supplier is rigorously assessed against a consistent set of measures. A scoring system is often a useful approach, with each of the evaluation criteria weighted with the suppliers' proposals

> ## KEY CONCEPT
>
> One of the hidden dangers of any e-business development is the potential for too great an emphasis on technology. What it can do, how exciting it is and why it's fabulous all too frequently take precedence over the need to focus clearly on customers. The best role for technology in the online environment remains as an enabler, adding value for the customer, and here it has few equals.

marked against measure. The winning supplier is the one that scores the highest (with the most significant issues weighted with the greatest score). One particular issue to consider when evaluating suppliers is the degree of risk associated with them. This covers a wide range of issues, from matching the number and scope of their personnel with the expertise that you require to their financial structure and the security of their operations.

- *Evaluating software applications* – when selecting an e-commerce web site application from a supplier, it is useful to consider its effectiveness across the following criteria:
  - *Layout and design of the site* – is the product flexible enough to allow users to manage and develop the look and feel of the site, adjusting its features and building

its effectiveness to suit the customer and the needs of the business?

- *Integration and flexibility* – how easy is it for the product to link and synchronise with other IT systems, enabling business processes to work smoothly, reliably and cost-effectively? For example, can employees add product information and images, and can customers order direct into the order-processing system, removing the need for manual intervention?
- *Product features* – is the system capable of applying advanced features, such as customisation, membership tracking or specialised pricing, as the business develops?
- *Site management and reporting* – does the system allow the user easily and routinely to view, manage, update and interrogate the site regularly, allowing business reports to be produced and synchronised with other systems (e.g. financial management software)?
- *Extendibility* – is the system able to grow with the needs of customers and the market, allowing the site to develop dynamically to take account of issues such as pricing, security and speed of service, for example?

These criteria can be used in a matrix form, with potential new systems scored against each of these measures.

3 Ensuring the success of the supplier management process

Making sure that suppliers and the supply chain process work as intended is a challenge for any organisation at the best of times, and online it is particularly demanding and fraught with potential problems and pitfalls for the unwary. The process clearly starts with knowing what you want and getting the best supplier to match it, as mentioned above.

Following on very closely from this is the need to negotiate the purchase successfully. A successful e-commerce negotiation has to deliver the following agreed outcomes:

♦ A clear understanding of the *vendor's costs*, including knowledge of how these are driven and how they can be reduced or increased. Payment terms and schedules are also important, particularly with large projects or smaller suppliers. It may also be worth considering incentives for the supplier to meet and exceed performance targets.

♦ Acceptance of a realistic *timetable for implementation*, including milestones in the implementation process focusing developments as well as allowing opportunities for review.

♦ Roles and responsibilities in the process, in particular explicit *recognition of the key areas of risk* and how these will be addressed. For e-commerce suppliers, risks may include technical failures, missed deadlines, lost business – due to poor performance – and a failure of the product to meet the required specification. Responsibilities and remedies in such situations need to be agreed. (It is also worth considering the need to build close, associative relations with suppliers, recognising that any person, system or organisation is fallible and that the important issue is to prevent difficulties arising and resolve them swiftly if they do.)

♦ Establish a *service-level agreement*, clearly and unequivocally detailing what level of service is expected on an on-going basis and what will be charged.

Common problems and pitfalls to avoid include the following:

♦ Not evaluating the software systems properly and selecting the wrong vendor or supplier.

♦ Purchasing unproven software or dealing with an unproven organisation.

♦ Buying solely on price – getting the cheapest solution.

♦ Not tying down the details and not benefiting from legal assistance and expertise.

♦ Failing to understand the supplier's issues, motives and concerns and ensuring that your project has the necessary level of commitment and support from the supplier.

♦ Failing to establish an adequate or workable service-level agreement.

♦ Avoiding external expertise – supplier selection, negotiation and management can be significantly enhanced with external expertise, providing a new perspective on the business.

♦ Paying too much for a software system, service or supply, or paying too much for on-going maintenance and support.

♦ Getting locked into an inflexible, long-term commitment that may be fine at the outset but becomes outdated, with little prospect of change or development.

♦ Failing to integrate the supplier or the system adquately into the business.

4 Monitoring progress and continuously enhancing the process: implementation

Once a supplier or system has been selected the next step, implementation, should follow easily, with the timetable, milestones and activities being fulfilled. It is important to bear in mind several other techniques to ensure success:

♦ *View all developments from the customer's standpoint.* Managing processes and information, cutting costs or improving profits may appear to work, but what do customers really think? Is their experience tangibly improved; if so, how exactly? If not, why and what can be done about it?

- *Involve all of the people affected by the new system or supplier.* Ask for their input, gain their confidence and support and evaluate their suggestions, taking action where these provide a better approach.

- *Understand where the organisation is vulnerable and weak,* those areas where its capabilities need to be developed, and act to improve these. Training and staff development are typical areas where further work and effort are required when changes are made to suppliers, the supply chain or business systems.

- *Monitor the implementation of the system,* and in particular establish information systems that will enable quick and effective decision making. It is also important to anticipate the work that will be needed to integrate back-office systems with front-end customer-facing systems. Understanding the short-term consequences of proposed changes to suppliers, the supply chain and systems is important and can form the basis for an action plan to counter immediate difficulties and issues.

- *Look for ways to enhance the system* – clearly, one of the most important methods of achieving this is by using online capabilities to assess customers' priorities, but the wealth of information and expertise that will have been acquired can also be used to powerful effect.

Managing knowledge to enhance profitability

CHAPTER 10

Overview

How organisations manage knowledge using the Internet, leveraging both tacit and explicit knowledge to create a superior organisation succeeding in all its activities, is a key driver of growth and profitability and an issue that is explored in this chapter. One of the greatest advantages of e-business is the explosion in knowledge across a broad range of areas including customers, markets and internal organisational developments. Managing this broad scope of expertise and knowledge can be accomplished in a way that brings competitive advantage, but it requires specific skills and techniques.

Knowledge and human capital are old concepts; what is new is the understanding that information and knowledge have to be defined, nurtured, developed, managed and used just like any other strategic resource or asset. Achieving this can provide cascading benefits throughout the organisation, delivering profitability at

---

CONTINUED ... Overview

every level. The information and knowledge that are latent within an organisation are valuable, often essential, resources for making decisions, solving problems and ensuring success. What is particularly important is that the role of information and knowledge is actively recognised, controlled and managed before, during and after the decision-making process. To help achieve this, this chapter will:

- Outline the main benefits to the e-business of managing knowledge and information.
- Explain how to manage knowledge in a way that helps in decision making and enhances profitability for the profit-driven e-business.
- Describe how to establish an effective information management framework, providing benefits for the customer and business in general.

The importance of knowledge and information management online

Knowledge is the *intellectual capital* that an organisation possesses. This is much more than data, as it includes the wealth of experience and expertise within an organisation. Increasingly, organisations are recognising the benefits of using all of their employees' skills and knowledge and this has become an essential resource for decision making that needs to be proactively managed. Furthermore, knowledge and information are pre-requisites for effective business decisions. As both elements are of such fundamental importance, it is valuable to have an effective, simple and robust system that allows information and expertise to flow freely to key points in the organisation where it can be used.

It is undeniable that both the quantity and quality of commercial information available to businesses have increased dramatically in a very short time, as a result of businesses going online. Indeed, the ability to gather detailed, comprehensive and personalised customer information is one of the main drivers of e-business growth and one of the biggest benefits for customers and opportunities for businesses. However, ensuring that the right information is available in the right place at the right time remains a major challenge. In addition, there is the complex, frequently overlooked yet important task of ensuring that traditional metrics and sources of information are enriched rather than buried as a result of the information explosion occurring in many e-businesses.

> **KEY CONCEPT**
>
> An information firestorm rages in every successful and developing business, and how it is managed can easily determine future success or failure. It is an inevitable natural consequence of trading online that can be leveraged to create new sources of competitive advantage, yet it is important to combine it with conventional performance indicators or the risk is that you will lose much of its value.

Information has both positive and negative aspects that relate to the decision making process. First, information affects people's judgement and behaviour and there can often be suspicion, frustration or resentment if information is withheld or ineffectively deployed. Second, information changes the way that people act, their responsibilities and the work they do. It can have a major effect on status, training needs, accountability and level of control and it can determine the way they approach management tasks of delegating, time management, recruiting, communicating and leading people, as well as decision making. Finally, introducing strategies and systems to control and direct information can also cause short-term upheavals that may be disruptive, causing additional work and pressure. The key to success is therefore to understand, plan and control the organisation's flow of information – as well as the expertise (or knowledge) contained within the business – so that it supports decision making.

 ## GETTING STARTED: four characteristics of Internet-derived information and their impact on business development

There are four characteristics of Internet-derived information that are critical to the discovery of new business opportunities:

All information is digital

The first and most obvious characteristic is that all information on the Internet must be in digital form; it can therefore be disseminated to a few people or many at the click of a mouse. Many e-business entrepreneurs have gone beyond this to claim that 'what can be digitised will be digitised', such as Jeffrey Dachis, founder and CEO of Razorfish.com. Finding out what customers need and how this can be digitised and supplied is a potential opportunity. Several educational publishers, for example, have realised that their end-users, students, would value help with their homework assignments, and they provide online guides and tutorials as a new business opportunity.

Information is costly to produce, but cheap to reproduce

Because of the disparity resulting from this characteristic of information, products must be priced according to what people will pay for them, rather than their cost of production.

In addition, since reproducing information products is cheap, they can be made available at very low marginal costs. This situation also enables businesses to focus their spend not on delivery but on other aspects of the business, such as selling and developing customer loyalty. It does, however, significantly alter the economics of the business. A danger of this situation is the possibility of information overload, the likelihood that data will simply overwhelm the business. The solution is to ensure that the necessary information is understood and made readily available.

Information needs to be sampled for people fully to appreciate its value and benefit

Information is what economists call an 'experience good'. Often (although not always) customers do not know whether they will find an information product useful until they try it. With experience goods the aim has to be to make samples widely available, with the aim of getting as many people as possible to try the product before they buy it. On the Internet, many companies have used push technologies to try to get prospects to sample their information goods and services and this in turn has led to a proliferation of aggressive tactics to move information to the customer's desktop. There is now a backlash against this aggressive approach (certainly in Europe) and the need is to achieve sampling without using such aggressive techniques.

People who are using information benefit from intermediaries

The fourth characteristic of information concerns the need for economising on accessing, collecting and using information. Customers online (in common with when they watch television or other media) usually have a limited attention span and time to search for and use information. In a world of abundant digital information, the need for focusing one's attention and time on the use of the right information at the right time creates an enormous business opportunity for infomediaries.

There are two main types of infomediary, the first being vendor-oriented infomediaries who aggregate customer information and transactions on behalf of companies want-

> **KEY CONCEPT**
>
> On the Internet there are many significant opportunities to help people and companies navigate for critical information that saves time, attention and money: help that can be provided by infomediaries. Infomediaries are people or companies who help others to focus on just the right information for their needs, saving and increasing time effectiveness.

ing to sell their products and services. They act either as lead generators or as audience brokers.

The second type of infomediary is customer oriented, acting on behalf of customers by seeking out information or completing transactions on the Internet. They come in several forms:

- the *filter*, who prevents unwanted marketing messages from reaching customers;
- the *agent* (such as the online stock trader E*TRADE or the ubiquitous Amazon.com) acting on behalf of customers to locate information of interest to them or carry out transactions on their behalf;
- the *proxy*, who acts on behalf of customers on the Web without revealing their identity. These services set up vendor relationships and offer their customers the opportunity to decide what they will or will not reveal about themselves.

These infomediaries succeed by generating trust in their customers, who must be willing to share information about themselves, their interests and their behaviours. The drivers of growth for customer-oriented infomediaries are twofold: to attract enough customers to build critical mass for their own business; and to generate sufficient transactions across diverse products and services to develop rich profiles of customer behaviours. These are of value to potential vendors who might wish to transact through the customer-oriented infomediary.

Managing knowledge to aid decision making and drive profitability

Assessing and managing the organisation's knowledge base

A frequently overlooked resource when making decisions is the knowledge base of the organisation: what people know and what they can do. The tendency is to rely either on technology or else on data flows and processes, with the result that the whole situation becomes dehumanised and the wealth of knowledge that individuals possess is disregarded. Avoiding this situation and gaining maximum benefit from this resource is the focus of knowledge management.

 GETTING STARTED: managing knowledge in the e-business to support decisions

There are several techniques that are helpful for managing knowledge to support decision making:

Undertaking a knowledge audit

Because knowledge is often overlooked, neglected or confined to one person (or a handful of people), it can often be difficult to assess. One possible solution is to undertake a knowledge audit with three core components.

- Define what knowledge assets exist in the organisation (specifically, what information or skills there are that would be difficult or expensive to replace).
- Locate those knowledge assets and who keeps (or 'owns') them.
- Classify the knowledge assets and see how they relate to other assets. It may be that the answer to one problem lies elsewhere in the organisation, unrecognised.

Increasing knowledge

Once the organisation has audited its knowledge base, it needs to match what it has with what the strategy – or functions of the organisation – requires. The task is to increase the knowledge base so that the organisation can achieve its aims. There are three core methods of expanding the knowledge base: buying knowledge by hiring staff, forming alliances and partnerships with other organisations, or outsourcing functions to organisations where the required expertise already exists; renting knowledge by hiring consultants or subcontracting work; developing knowledge by training people and creating opportunities within the organisation to support continuous learning.

In addition, it is important to assess the information requirements that you will want from your web site or, if it is already established, how it might be further refined and enhanced to deliver new sources of information.

Maintaining knowledge

Avoiding 'knowledge gaps' in an organisation is a constant struggle, but one that is important in ensuring that decisions are made and implemented well. In recent years downsizing (redundancy) programmes have highlighted the dangers of removing people with expertise and experience, and down-sized organisations often find that they lose a great deal of valuable knowledge, experience and skills that had not previously been taken into account, with significant implications for decision making, problem solving and innovation. Given the steady turnover in e-business professionals, it is important to codify, capture and store people's expertise and tacit knowledge.

Recognising and exploiting knowledge

Often it is difficult to recognise the value and potential of knowledge for decision making or problem solving. A knowledge audit will help, but perhaps more fundamentally, than that a change in attitude will be important. Consider *who* can help with the decision, *what* they have to offer and *how* people need to be developed to handle bigger decisions. It is also worth remembering that if there are knowledge gaps, the online environment makes it much, much easier than ever before to remedy the situation.

Protecting knowledge

Knowledge falls into two categories: explicit knowledge, such as copyright or information codified in handbooks, systems or procedures, and tacit knowledge, which is retained by individuals and includes learning, experience, observation, deduction and informally acquired knowledge. Both types of knowledge are valuable for decision making and need to be nurtured and protected. Explicit knowledge can be protected through legal procedures; although tacit knowledge can also be protected by legal methods (such as non-compete clauses in employment contracts), this is usually unsatisfactory. A better approach is to ensure that the relevant knowledge is recorded and passed on, requiring efficient succession planning.

Being prepared: establishing an effective information management framework

Devising an information management framework

Devising an efficient system for managing information makes decision making much easier. It enables managers and others routinely to plan, co-ordinate and control the information that is produced, as well as where and when it flows. There are several issues to consider when developing a management information system. First, consider what information is needed, perhaps preparing a wish list of information to improve decisions and achieve objectives. It can also be helpful to group information into different types, such as aggregated customer information, specific customer details and preferences for future developments. Often, reviewing data for an area of activity, such as markets and customers, helps to put each decision into perspective, as well as ensuring that all the necessary information is available.

Second, understand when information is required. Too much data produced too frequently can result in information overload, making it harder to discern trends or relevant details.

The next issue is to ensure that you know who requires the information. Just because information is superfluous to one person does not mean it is worthless, it may be exactly what someone else needs for their decisions! Intranets and extranets between people who need to share information are invaluable tools and are often provided as built-in features of web site or e-mail software. They can help to ensure that people are receiving the information they need and that it is not simply passing them by.

Knowing who requires each item of information can also mean assessing *how* information flows through the organisation. Often information flows according to status: from the top to the bottom of the organisation along the channels of the organisation chart. Clearly, this is not always the most effective route and there are inherent weaknesses; for example, some people may require more

> ## KEY CONCEPT
>
> Consider not only what information is required, but how best to display information derived from the business. For people to use information easily it need to be clear and accessible and it is important to get the balance right: too much data is distracting and too little is often inadequate.

data, or more time with the data, than others. The solution may be to reorganise information flows or to put in place systems providing wide access to relevant information. A better information flow is usually to and from the customer.

Avoiding the potential pitfalls of information systems

There are several potential problems faced by most businesses when developing and implementing information systems:

- *Ensuring security of information.* Confidential data needs to be secure; furthermore, information used for decisions needs to be backed up in a foolproof way, so that, in a worst-case disaster, valuable information would not be lost.
- *Managing costs and ensuring that the required level of support is provided.* To gain maximum value from an investment in information technology, it often helps to list all of the functions and features that are required (including price and support) and ensure that these minimum requirements are fulfilled.

- *Integrating information into the organisational culture.* Throughout the organisation, information needs to be welcomed for the benefits it provides, rather than resented or simply ignored. Often this means listening and accepting the wishes of the people using the systems, resolving any problems or concerns they may have.

- *Understanding and meeting the e-business's legal requirements,* particularly as these increase in scope and complexity. Legal issues need to be clearly understood when establishing systems for managing information.

- *Incorrectly interpreting and using information.* Unwittingly or otherwise, data can be misinterpreted and misused; people not only make errors in judgement, but can use data to support false conclusions and actions.

 GETTING STARTED: establishing an effective information management framework (the information life cycle)

Understanding how information flows, what it is used for and the ways in which it is applied to decision making can be very useful in managing information. It may be useful to think of information as going through a cycle, as in Figure 10.1.

Clearly, the uses of information blend into each other, but in organising the flow of information for decision making it can help to think in terms of separate stages, each with its own characteristics and techniques.

1 Understanding the business's information requirements

Knowing what information is needed is a vital pre-requisite for ensuring that it is routinely available, consistent and

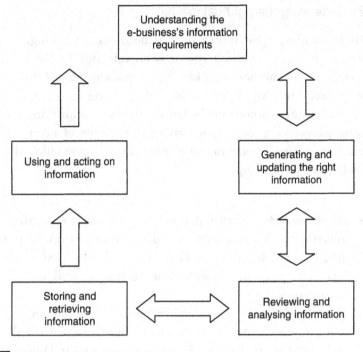

Figure 10.1: The information life cycle

reliable. It is worth asking colleagues and subordinates (and possibly customers too) key questions to help understand information requirements, for example:

- what information is needed;
- how it should be presented;
- when it needs to be supplied – timing and frequency;
- where it comes from on the web site or in the organisation – this is often useful in determining the quality of information as well as relevant details that may help to put the facts in context;
- what restrictions there are – for example, whether it contains confidential financial details;
- which decisions and activities it supports.

2   Generating the right data

Understanding what information is needed is one thing, getting it – and ensuring that it is reliable and 'fit for purpose' – is another. The key is to approach the task in two ways: acquiring the information and verifying it.

Techniques to consider when seeking and acquiring information vary hugely, according to the type of information required. Some popular approaches to generating data include the following:

- *Desk research* – questionnaires, surveys, telephone calls, meetings and interviews, as well as other sources such as libraries and information centres can all prove extremely valuable, providing insights and analysis as well as information.
- *Interrogating online sources of information,* including the company web site or the Internet (many companies sell information services online, such as Reuters or Dun and Bradstreet) providing relevant, accessible information that is regularly updated.
- *Networking* (asking and giving help to colleagues and contacts, old and new) is an approach that has gained in popularity and acceptance, as people realise that helping others can also mean helping oneself.

Depending on the sensitivity of the information required, people are generally flattered to be asked for information and they are usually pleased to be able to help. Asking people who have experienced a similar situation can be very useful, if only for building confidence, while asking those who have never encountered the situation before can also help as it provides objectivity. Of course, the best approach depends entirely on the nature of the decision to be made.

3 Reviewing and analysing information

Analysing information is a separate discipline in itself and there are many quantitative methods that will help in making sense of information, highlighting trends as well as anomalies. Furthermore, the process of reviewing and analysing information is invariably the starting point for solving the problem or finding the best decision. The review process not only enables possible options to emerge, but can be used to scrutinise them and rate their effectiveness.

There are many rules and standards that should be employed to ensure that analysis of information is rigorous, although the guiding principle when analysing information for decision making is to maintain objectivity. Objectivity will help to ensure that the decision is fair, logical and practical, and this is particularly important for complex decisions. However, using information to justify a predetermined course of action is largely a waste of time. If you have already decided and made up your mind, it is surely better to spend your energies taking action than to look for some justification that may or may not exist.

Challenging the information – asking why something is the way it appears – is a further important step in analysing the information, formulating ideas, removing assumptions and generating practical, workable solutions.

In addition to quantitative and statistical analysis, scenario planning, modelling and simulation are useful techniques that generate information for decision making by trying out different options. The key is to try to create the most realistic set of circumstances possible, perhaps by trial and error, and take account of as many variables as possible.

4 Storing and retrieving data

This stage of the information life cycle is difficult to keep in balance: often it is either totally overlooked or disproportionately emphasised. The following elements are important when storing and retrieving information for decision making:

- Information needs to be widely accessible for use by those who need it, at the point of use.
- It needs to be clearly labelled and categorised so that it is understood by those using it. A thesaurus or dictionary of terms can be a useful technique for classifying information.
- It needs to be relevant, up to date and fit for purpose. This means establishing criteria for adding new information and discarding (or archiving) old details that may no longer be relevant.
- It needs to be cost-effective – it is not unheard of for massive computer systems serviced by highly trained, talented people to grow within an organisation, out of all proportion to the needs of the task. Using a sledgehammer to crack a nut is rarely cost-effective!

5 Using and acting on information

The final stage of the information life cycle is to use the information to generate ideas, formulate plans, reach conclusions and decide. This last stage pulls together the preceding parts of the process and, as the decision is implemented, the cycle starts again, with additional information requirements being identified.

The following techniques are useful for managing information during this last stage:

- *Monitor decisions* – identify and use sources of information to monitor how well the decision is being implemented. This will help to assess whether new decisions are necessary and whether the information for future choices needs to change.

- *Act methodically* – information needs to be used as a tool and managed objectively throughout the decision-making process. Often this is difficult to sustain, but the danger is that decisions taken during the final implementation of the decision will be wrong, undermining the outcome.
- *Manage time constraints and pressures that may exist* – certain situations require fast decisions, but the key is not to be bullied by information. Instead, maintain a clear, level-headed understanding of the goals required and the approach needed to achieve them.

It is important to note that information often flows in both directions (as indicated by the double arrows on the right-hand side of Figure 10.1) and that information may need to be verified by referring back to the previous stage.

For further detailed analysis and solutions to the question of managing knowledge, refer to Sultan Kermally's book *New Economy Energy: Unleashing Knowledge for Competitive Advantage*, also in the New Economy Excellence series.

Financial techniques to reduce costs, minimise risk and boost profits online

CHAPTER 11

Overview

This chapter looks at some of the technical financial tools for profitable e-business management. It is tempting to think that a focus on customers and markets will immediately translate into profitability and success. While this is a pre-requisite for a successful e-business, a common-sense approach to standard financial issues of cost control, risk management and profit maximisation is also essential.

There is a wide range of financial management techniques for enhancing profitability, which need to be applied effectively to e-business and online trading conditions. This chapter will therefore highlight key issues and potential solutions to boost profits and enhance financial effectiveness, including:

CONTINUED . . . **Overview**

- cost-reduction techniques;
- evaluating and managing financial risk for an e-business.

Cost-reduction techniques
Avoiding the 'tomorrow syndrome'

All too often e-businesses are swept along by their own hype. For example, net entrepreneurs proclaim that market share is all, believing that it doesn't matter if the business makes a loss in the short or medium term, because as long as market share is being delivered this will, in time, translate into massive profitability. The truth is, of course, that it may. It may also be the case that *tomorrow* online sales suddenly increase by a factor of ten, competitors disappear, and the tooth fairy, Easter Bunny and March Hare all get together to set up their own interactive web site! There are several arguments against this tomorrow syndrome.

First, promises may not come true. This is true for any business at any time, and believing that common-sense business logic does not apply for online businesses is a grave error. Errors can easily be made – online more than anywhere else – and a business model relying entirely on optimistic prediction is terribly flawed. Second, businesses that do not focus on their current profitability may simply not last until tomorrow, when success is predicted and when it may actually emerge. In particular, cash-flow problems, stakeholder concerns or both may combine to sink the business, before the promised 'jam tomorrow' is reached. Third, if the business is running at a loss or a little above break-even, its room for manoeuvre is greatly reduced. This matters in any market, for any business, at any time; but in the highly charged, competitive and dynamic online environment, it can be critical to success or failure.

Simply put, online businesses need some cash reserves to ensure that they can compete and adapt. It is also the case that a lack of cash or financial flexibility can deliver a self-fulfilling prophecy: businesses may enter the market knowing that all they have to do is last longer than their online competitor. All the new entrant needs is a competitive (but not necessarily better) value proposition – and deeper pockets that can fund the business for longer.

The final argument against the tomorrow syndrome concerns expense: developing and managing a web site is not cheap. Web sites cost money, and to have a large amount of expenditure supposedly financed by future revenues and without adequate financial planning, resources or controls is a weak if not disastrous position from which to start.

A first step in avoiding the tomorrow syndrome is to manage and reduce costs and a number of online cost-reduction initiatives can be employed:

- Product profitability analysis.
- Eliminating waste and non-core activities (ensuring lean operations).
- Structuring your organisation so that it is flat, flexible and customer focused.
- E-business cost planning (particularly target costing and continuous improvement costing).

To realise the full potential of these measures requires the development of new approaches to information collection and presentation. This is easier to accomplish in the online world, where precise customer information should be readily available.

Product profitability analysis

The proliferation of products that exist in an increasingly competitive online business environment – coupled with simple, historically based cost-assignment methods – will inevitably result in inaccurate product profitability information leading to poor decisions. The solution is a rational process of analysing product profitability.

This process starts with *understanding product costs*. Assigning overhead costs fairly and accurately has always been a challenge for any business, not simply an e-business. There are innumerable examples of product cost analyses that have demonstrated that classical, simple overhead cost assignments can be very misleading. However, in recent years a number of companies have undertaken activity-based costing (ABC) initiatives intended to assign overhead costs more effectively to products, in order to ascertain more about relative product cost and profit performance. Such a process yields several major benefits, including a better understanding of what drives costs in a business. Such characteristics as product complexity, the number of outside vendors, the number of purchase orders, the nature of production processes and special customer requirements are the principal drivers of product costs. With this analysis, the e-business is better placed to make changes that influence the drivers and resultant costs.

The second major benefit from product cost and profit analysis is an enhanced understanding of which parts of the web site make more money and which make less – or even lose money. There are examples of businesses who, after they have done an ABC profitability analysis, concluded that there are a number of products whose price, cost and volume characteristics are such that they lose money. After dropping the losing products from the product line, overall profitability and customer responsiveness online improved.

The next part of the process is to *avoid the pitfalls of overhead cost assignment.* When online competition increases products proliferate, product life cycles shorten, product development and marketing expenses go up and prices (and discounts) may alter. In this dynamic environment it is also entirely possible to allocate costs misleadingly. Furthermore, most product cost systems virtually ignore the cost of carrying inventory. Some of the carrying costs such as warehousing, delivery and insurance costs may be included in the overhead cost structure and get related to products, but not to the right products. The financial costs of carrying inventory are ignored in the product cost calculation process. If some products move through the production process quickly and others move through more slowly, resulting in higher inventories and costs, and if these differences are not identified and considered in product costing, the accuracy of product costing is reduced.

The next stage, *ensuring that there are adequate information systems* for effective product cost and profitability analysis, is vital. If the information regarding online overheads is pooled in such a way that it is difficult to assign to particular products, the ability to determine product costs and profitability – and therefore to make rational business decisions – is

> ## KEY CONCEPT
>
> For those businesses combining a physical presence with an online one (so-called clicks and mortar businesses), ensuring that overhead costs are accurately assigned is fundamentally important. However, of equal relevance is the need to ensure that this process is responsive and dynamic, as customer relationships develop and affect both environments.

compromised. If certain costs such as research, engineering, development, distribution and sales are driven by different product characteristics but are not captured in the products' costs, decisions may also be misdirected. While it is easy to know what a customer buys, knowing *how much* and *how frequently* a particular customer buys is often a problem in the offline world, particularly if that customer buys products from more than one operating unit. Online, it is important to ensure that personalised customer purchase data is captured and used.

Capturing all of the costs of the online business is also decisive and harder than it may appear. There are a number of other costs in addition to product costs, usually referred to as operating expenses or period costs. These are not captured in the product cost definition and are probably more related to market and individual customer distinctions than to product lines and products. To understand customer profitability fully these costs have to be attached to individual customers. Different commission rates, discounts and other allowances, advertising and promotion expenses, field support and customer service may be driven by customer characteristics rather than product. If there are differences in a customer's demands on an organisation, the cost implications need to be understood and captured.

To enhance profitability, business managers need to focus on customer groups depending on the turnover and profitability they provide. *High-volume, high-profit* customers are the ones who need to be maintained. Put another way, online there may be many unprofitable, time-wasting customers who do not provide a business with much of its overall profitability. Those customers who fall in the *low-volume, high-profit* category need to be developed so their volume increases. This may be accomplished through additional effort or some price/volume trade-offs. The *high-volume, low-profit* customers have to be managed in a different way. It needs to be understood why they fall into that category. For instance, is it because of the nature of the mix of products they buy? This kind of information permits these three customer groups to be managed. Using online technology it is feasible to understand what each customer buys, when and even why – and to use this information to develop your activities so that you drive customers to the more profitable parts of the business.

Eliminating waste and non-core activities: ensuring lean operations

Eliminating waste

The objective of product profitability analysis is to determine what it really costs to produce and serve different markets and customers. The decision to eliminate certain unprofitable products and customers can reduce costs and may improve profitability. However, activity-based thinking also enables e-businesses to reduce costs markedly in other ways. For many years leading Japanese companies have directed much of their cost management efforts toward *muda* or waste elimination, and the concepts of just in time (JIT), process analysis, process mapping and re-engineering became a part of business thinking even before the Internet revolution. Process analysis thinks of the activities of a business as a chain of events, perhaps from the beginning of the manufacturing process through to the end, and breaks down the chain of activities into discrete, yet identifiable tasks. Assigning activity costs to each part of a process will help to highlight those areas where costs are too high in relation to customers and revenue.

Ensuring lean operations

Waste elimination is primarily generated and focused within the organisation. It starts with the belief that there is unnecessary activity in typical processes, particularly for the e-business migrating from the offline world. This waste can be eliminated by such structural changes as rearranging facilities and eliminating unnecessary work and resources.

Furthermore, the lean operations perspective starts with the view that everything a business does should be customer driven and that virtually nothing should be done until customers demand it. If an activity is not wanted or needed by the customer, and the customer would not pay for it because it has no value, that activity should not be done. For those products and specific activities that are important to the customer, response has to be very quick. Lean companies think in terms of *pulling* products or services out of an organisation, rather than *pushing* them through. In a highly competitive online environment one way in which an e-business may differentiate itself is to be very responsive to the unique demands of individual customers. The supplier must be able to produce a variety of products and services quickly, at low cost. That requires the flexibility to respond quickly.

Focusing on efficient business processes and work flows

It is also worth considering how work can flow around the e-business so that it is efficient and may actually reduce costs. The danger for the e-business is that support functions such as accounting or order processing may be developed entirely from the old, offline model, ignoring the potential for new cost savings (or customer opportunities). Many successful businesses have taken traditionally paper-intensive areas as purchasing and rearranged them, ensuring that the work flows from one person to another in a quick, efficient fashion rather than in batches from one function to another. Several finance organisations have applied process analysis to such activities as credit approval, accounts payables, payroll, collections and even their general ledger accounting and monthly closing activities. What is needed is a complete change in thinking regarding the purpose of cost systems and information. Instead of focusing on inventory valuation and financial reporting, the focus needs to shift to cost reduction and cost assignment for decision-making purposes.

Developing flexibility and reducing set-up times

Once the revised processes are lined up, in order and close together to minimise the waste, it becomes important to build flexibility into the process such that a variety of customer demands may be quickly and easily met. This requires significant focus on reducing set-up time. Information regarding set-up times and cost is not a typical component of many companies' information systems. Set-up costs may include people, materials and equipment, and these may be scattered throughout the financial accounts. Without knowing what these costs are – and what drives them – managers are unable to focus on this critical element of customer-focused, high-speed response capability.

For the profit-driven e-business, much of the information normally used in more traditional environments, such as forecasts of future expectations, become less necessary. If the various stages of a process are clearly linked, demand at one stage triggers the appropriate demand at the previous stage and so on. Furthermore, new information may be realised as very important.

Structuring your organisation so that it is flat, flexible and customer focused

Many profitable e-businesses have shifted from the economies of scale model so that support activities (such as purchasing, scheduling, inventory control, plant engineering, maintenance, quality control and plant accounting) are embedded in lines of business. What this does is make indirect, and difficult to trace, costs directly identifiable to the lines and therefore much more traceable.

Outsourcing

The benefits of outsourcing non-core functions were explored in greater detail in Chapter 10. However, it is worth noting that purchasing departments are often measured on their ability to buy cheaply and beat standard costs. This has resulted in large orders, excess inventory, additional storage facilities, greater insurance and the risk of product damage and obsolescence. Beating price frequently comes with a cost, which might be lower quantity. This may result in production problems, rework costs and delivery delays. Making purchasing an integral part of the business team results in an entirely different attitude: buying what is needed, when it is needed to meet end-customer needs and expectations.

Information requirements for flat organisations

E-businesses need to have flat organisation structures to ensure that they are flexible, responsive and customer focused. Profitable e-businesses have concluded that their focus should be horizontal, helping to meet customer needs, rather than vertical, which may suit the organisation. In addition, information should flow from customers into the business, and a timely response should flow from the business to customers. This puts a different focus on information needs and organisational staffing.

Major corporations such as General Electric have flattened their organisations so that the group, business unit and division staffs have been markedly reduced. Whole layers of organisations have been removed and those near the top of the organisation become closer to where the action is happening. Activity and process analysis, emphasis on the customer, cleaning out waste and emphasising focus and flat structures collectively represent huge cost-saving opportunities. For many businesses, as much as 10 to 20 per cent of all costs can be reduced.

E-business cost planning: target costing and continuous improvement costing

Most of the costs of an e-business are determined during the early product planning and development phase. Yet most cost management, control and reduction efforts are applied *later* in the web site's development, when suppliers are chosen, architecture is set and the site is online. This is locking the barn door after the horse has bolted.

Target costing

One solution is to reverse the cost management process, so that market prices and predetermined profit margins are used to drive costs. As the e-business concept and design stages are developing, representatives from different business functions (such as engineering, manufacturing, finance, marketing, sales and service) get involved to ensure that the product concept and design decisions are made with the broadest perspective in mind. The intention is that the business model for the web site meets, or beats, the requirements in the marketplace, favourably influencing material costs, capital investment requirements, business processes and overall costs, and achieving the targeted profit margin.

The information requirements for this target costing approach are significantly different to those for the more traditional 'cost plus' model. It is necessary for an e-business to have accurate information regarding its customers' wants and needs in terms of functionality, price and comparable competitive product information. Many companies spend little or no time trying to understand customers' future wants and needs, what customers consider the most important attributes of the products or services they are considering and *how much* customers are willing to pay for them. The real irony is that online, this is so easy to achieve and one of the greatest benefits of the Internet. Sadly, many companies have virtually no information regarding competitive products and services, what functions are offered, how they differ and at what price they are offered. Without this kind of information, it is virtually impossible to establish the target price relative to the products and functions to be offered.

Continuous improvement costing

There is a clear distinction between target costing, taking significant costs out of products and processes during the product concept and development phases, and continuous improvement or *kaizen* costing, driven by the necessity to make profits in a market-driven pricing environment. One way that profitable e-businesses accomplish continuous improvement costing is to institute a culture of continuous cost reduction. One method of achieving this, first favoured by Japanese companies, is to encourage employees to suggest ways to improve the business. Reducing costs becomes everyone's job in such a cultural environment and the nature of an e-business, where ideally everyone should feel some sense of ownership, understanding and affinity with their dot-com, is particularly well suited to this. The intent is not just arbitrarily to reduce costs, but to do so in the context of the larger business picture, meeting price in the marketplace, having the resources to reinvest, making money and building a business for the future.

To achieve major cost reductions requires a review of the whole process of planning, budgeting, reporting and analysis. This is so that instead of looking backward, comparing how one has performed relative to a pre-determined estimate or standard, the favoured approach is forward thinking, driven by customers online with constantly improving analysis leading to new insights, reduced costs and assets and increased economic value.

Evaluating and managing financial risk for an e-business

There are many worthy and valuable attributes when working in a profit-driven e-business, for example a refreshing focus on customers and innovation, and a dynamic approach generally. However, one of the downsides of this is a tendency for many e-businesses either to be over-exuberant, minimising or completely overlooking issues of financial risk on the grounds that it will all come good in time, or to demonstrate a lack of exuberance. This is where normally dynamic entrepreneurs avoid fulfilling the potential offered online because they are scared of the environment, believing it to be prohibitively expensive, risky or both. The solution is to take a pragmatic, detailed financial approach, so that the entrepreneur can evaluate the proposition and clearly understand:

- where the risks lie online;
- where the financial opportunities are and how to realise them;
- how to monitor, manage and control financial developments.

 IMPLEMENTATION CHECKLIST: six steps for evaluating and managing financial risk online

1 Review current business processes to understand how online developments will enhance profitability

There is a great deal of woolly and unsubstantiated thinking when considering e-business activities. It is important for senior managers to know how e-business activities will enhance the organisation's cash flows, and this can be achieved in the following ways:

◆ Establishing a baseline position, i.e. what the organisation's profitability would be without the proposed online developments, maintaining the status quo.

◆ Assessing the efficiency of the business's current processes, in particular how key aspects of the product proposition that are of value to the customer (e.g. delivery lead time or service support) can be improved. This is often achieved by asking as wide a group of people as possible, giving particular emphasis to those nearest to the customer.

2 Understand the key drivers in the e-business, both revenue and cost

The next step is to map out *how* the key aspects can be enhanced: what needs to be achieved, who would do it, how much would it cost, what would be the costs of disruption? Two areas of questioning are important here: what are the key drivers of revenue and cost in the business, and how will online developments affect these? This requires a detailed appraisal of all the activities, online and offline, to be completed, as well as a detailed assessment of the cost of these new enhancements and the likely benefits in terms of increased market share, increased prices and/or reduced cost.

In considering this, it can often help to approach the business from an entirely new, objective perspective, perhaps even developing a different business model. To this end, business consultants (a much maligned profession!) can add real value, questioning revered tenets of conventional wisdom and providing a dynamic perspective that is flexible, realistic and action oriented.

3 Develop a project plan for the e-business

By this stage the following elements should have been prepared:

- A base case for the finances of the business without any online developments (i.e. maintaining the status quo).
- A map of the current business processes, highlighting areas where these can be enhanced to add value to the customer, reduce cost for the business or both. This may even result in a new business model or approach.
- Information that quantifies the likely costs and benefits: a profitability projection.

The next stage is to develop the project plan for delivering these improvements. This should typically include details of:

- What needs to be done.
- Who will lead each stage and who will be involved.
- The time required for each stage.
- The cost assigned to each part of the process.
- The payment schedule (when completing a financial analysis the timing of expense payments makes a significant difference to the calculations of present value).

4   Develop a financial plan for the e-business

The financial plan needs to confirm the costs for each stage of the project. There is a range of financial management measures and techniques that can be used here – from key performance indicators to ratio analysis – but the main point is to understand how the business can deliver more value at less cost for the customer.

> **KEY CONCEPT**
>
> It is important to recognise and remember the unquestionable, enduring and all-pervading truths about developing your business on the Internet: it costs money and is rarely inexpensive, and usually the costs are underestimated and the savings or benefits over-emphasised.

One of the key aspects of the financial plan is an integrated cash-flow forecast for the e-business, highlighting the key areas where cash will come from and go to. These are incremental changes, over and above those that would have been incurred had the system remained unchanged, and they include the following:

◆ *Cash outflows for building the proposed e-commerce system* or making the proposed enhancements. Included in this section will be the cost of internal and external project staff; hardware, software and telecommunications costs; training costs; and, if the project results in job losses and reduced headcount, the costs of redundancy or transfer.

◆ *Incremental on-going cash outflows for operating the system.* The main cost elements here should be understood clearly at the outset of the project and many of the on-going costs can be fixed in a service-level agreement with external suppliers. Typically included in this cost category are software upgrades, insurance, security and trading costs (e.g. credit card merchant costs). Also significant are the need to modify business systems to take account of the new online activities and the need, for example, to recruit new staff or adapt the business processes to deliver greater flexibility for customers. It is worth highlighting the extent to which these are incremental costs, over and above those that would have been spent on the existing system.

◆ *Cash inflows from additional revenue streams* are often overlooked, yet these can be among the biggest advantages of using the Internet to redefine your business model. An example of this would be a business publishing company that now not only provides hard-copy information *ordered* via the Internet and the same data delivered via the Internet, but also offers the opportunity to customise the data, as well as to receive regular updates for a monthly subscription. The last two activities highlight the opportunities presented by the Internet for new revenue streams that were simply not as easy or accessible even as recently as ten years ago.

◆ *Cash inflows from reduced costs* are one of the most frequently mentioned benefits of online activities. The areas of potential cost saving are vast, with some of the most significant including reduced headcount and increased automation; reduced inventory and leaner production times generally through greater use of information; and an ability to forecast and schedule activities that can in turn be translated into lower prices from suppliers.

Developing a financial plan moves the business from evaluating the financial risk to managing that risk. The next two steps assume that the financial plan has been approved and that online developments are proceeding.

5 Monitor the financial performance

In most businesses there is a delicate balance between delivering a competitive business value proposition and maximising profits. E-businesses are certainly no different, although because of the pace and scope of change in the online world it is more important than ever to understand and monitor the key financial indicators and issues affecting profitability. It is perhaps an irony that the source of change and inherent instability, the online environment, also holds the key to the business's salvation: the facility rapidly and routinely to assemble and analyse critical business information and data. These are often described in the form of key performance indicators (KPIs) relating to customers, markets, prices, competitors, products, key trends and costs.

Effective monitoring requires the following:

- Agreement about what measures need to be monitored, how frequently, and what degree of variance from the norm requires further analysis.
- A clear understanding of who is responsible.
- The necessary tools to capture and analyse information.

6 Establish responsive and flexible processes for gathering financial information and making swift decisions

Once the processes are in place to monitor the key performance indicators, the next step is to ensure that there is a flat, empowered management structure with clearly defined roles and responsibilities, which will deliver clear direction and act swiftly and decisively when necessary. If this is not in place, the financial risk rises dramatically. Any business, particularly one that sets out to thrive in the online environment, needs to be able to provide clear processes for problem solving and decision making. If this is recognised at the start of online developments, the Web can be a remarkably helpful and valuable tool.

Resource building: the key to the competitive online business

CHAPTER 12

Overview

If cash is the lifeblood of a business, then resources are the central nervous system: the essential foundation that enables the business to move forward. Building resources provides the key to gaining and maintaining competitiveness. Customers, brand, suppliers, products, staff, intellectual property and many other resources can all be leveraged in unique, flexible and innovative ways to deliver an attractive and highly competitive value proposition.

This chapter outlines techniques for developing resources in order to *strengthen* the online organisation, ensuring that strategic objectives are achieved and advantage over business competitors is established. It also outlines the principles for using e-commerce to create competitive advantage.

Resource building

Resource building means developing the capability to achieve the organisation's goals but, more than that, developing resources is the key to achieving and sustaining competitive advantage. As was discussed in Chapter 8 on the subject of product innovation, if one business accumulates more and better resources than its competitors it has a clear and decisive advantage. For the online business, building a strong, pre-eminent competitive position involves resource building. This means both finding and developing resources – tangible and intangible – that will make the business more competitive. To achieve this, the most effective approach is often to build on existing strengths and resources rather than to develop new ones.

Types of resource

The scope of assets that can be regarded as resources is huge: any factor providing value or benefit to the organisation, from whatever origin, is a resource. Resources can typically be classified into two of four categories: either direct or indirect and tangible or intangible. *Direct* resources are those factors such as staff expertise, cash or intellectual property that can be developed and nurtured by the business. However, customers are perhaps the biggest single direct resource. (Viewing customers as a resource can be valuable in focusing ideas about how to accumulate and retain them.) *Indirect* resources are those factors that have a bearing on the quality, strength and value of resources. For example, effective training and development policies are indirect resources, as they build the effectiveness of staff expertise.

Tangible resources are those that can be physically seen, such as cash, inventory, sales volumes and customers, and these typically have the highest profile within the organisation as they are the most apparent. However, *intangible* resources such as service quality, brand reputation or staff expertise are also vital to success, if less obvious.

☑ IMPLEMENTATION CHECKLIST: developing resources for the online business

1 Determine which resources are key to success

The first step in resource building is to identify clearly those factors that will be most important in executing the business strategy online. Assessing which resources are important means taking a view across the whole of the business – online and offline – and identifying those factors, direct or indirect, tangible or intangible, which can be expanded and used for competitive advantage. This can mean mapping the resource base of the company and, in particular, asking questions such as:

- ◆ What resources useful for the online business does the organisation control at the moment?
- ◆ What new resources are needed to achieve success and to fulfil our strategic aims?
- ◆ What are the priorities for these new resources? This is particularly relevant as accumulating one resource is likely to affect – and possibly deplete – other resources.
- ◆ How can we acquire new resources? In particular, how can the web site be used to develop new resources and strengthen existing ones?

Underlying all of these issues is the question of relativity: the resource base needs to be effective *in relation to* the organisation's competitors.

2   Understand the nature of each resource

Understanding the resources essential for success requires a level of sophistication that goes beyond simply selling more of one type of product or service. Understanding the nature of each resource is important both for acquiring and maintaining resources and this means considering the following factors:

- *The fragility of the resource* – cash, quality, customers, staff, reputation and most other resources can all disappear with remarkable speed and ease. It is therefore important to understand and control the main factors likely to damage or undermine resources. For example, cash is the most obvious example of a resource that needs to be monitored and controlled, but other resources benefit from regular, rigorous monitoring and analysis. In addition, quality can be undermined by suppliers, service can be undermined by the attitudes of personnel and brand reputation may be damaged by the actions of distributors (consciously or otherwise).
- *Interaction between resources* – resources can combine to accelerate their growth in a virtuous cycle. For example, rising sales volumes may lead to more cash and more market share, both of which can be used to generate increasing sales, perhaps by entering new markets and so on. Similarly, product quality (an intangible resource) may lead to increased sales and this in turn can generate sufficient cash to continue improving product quality and continue increasing sales. In the same way that resources can interact to reinforce each other, they can also interact by *limiting* each other. For example, sales volumes may rise, but if the company is unable to increase production without reducing quality standards that resource (quality) will suffer, with potential consequences for other

resources (such as brand reputation and long-term sales). It is therefore worth considering which resources can help to build stocks of other resources.

◆ *Quality of resources* – it is important to consider in depth how the quality of resources can be developed. For example, a customer base is a valuable resource, but its *quality* might be improved by increasing customer loyalty to your brand, for instance by using customer loyalty schemes.

3 Focus on the timing of resource building

Market and competitive pressures can dictate not only *how* resources are accumulated, but also *when* is most favourable. It is also worth considering how *robust* are the resources: will they fade away with time, or will they simply become irrelevant? Invariably, there will be time lags between getting resources and using them: the key is therefore to anticipate when they will be needed and to develop them when that need arises.

4 Decide how best to build critical resources

Once the main resource requirements for the business have been identified and the areas for further development prioritised, the next stage is to develop the plans for building those resources. Questions to consider include:

◆ How have other organisations developed this resource (either competitors in the same industry or organisations in other industries, perhaps at other times)?
◆ What are the obstacles to resource accumulation and how can they be overcome?
◆ Can we use existing resources to develop new ones?

Using e-commerce to build resources

Understanding the competitive commercial environment online

One of the most celebrated theories of competitive strategy was developed by Professor Michael Porter, who identified five forces affecting competition in an industry. Of these, *industry rivalry*, direct competition resulting from the activities of companies in the same industry, is very often the most obvious and prominent source of competition.

The four other competitive factors affecting profitability are external to the industry. These are worth considering from the perspective of how they affect your online business activities. *Market entry* – the threat of potential new entrants to the market – is a major source of competition. *Who* might enter the market, *how* and *when* are significant factors affecting an organisation's tactics. Invariably the entire offer (including a range of factors such as quality and product features, as well as price) provided by the new entrant can challenge those already in the market.

Substitutability is the notion that businesses with products or services that may be substituted for others can face competition, especially over price. One possible counter to this is the approach first mentioned by Theodore Levitt in the 1960s, when he warned of the dangers of marketing myopia, or seeing one's business in simple, narrow terms, rather than from the perspective of the market. Just as a rail company, for example, can become a transportation company, so a publishing company can become an information provider in the new economy age.

The *bargaining power of suppliers* is another source of competition, accepting that suppliers are powerful if the item they provide is scarce and there are only a few suppliers, or if the item is unique. One potential solution here may be to build close, associative relations with core suppliers to secure delivery. In the long term, for certain businesses, the solution may be to move into the supplier's industry in order to safeguard supplies.

Finally, the *bargaining power of customers* is another competitive force. According to Porter there are several factors affecting the power of customers. These include the size and frequency of the customer's order, the ease with which customers can move to another supplier, the customer's knowledge of the business's competitors as well as the conditions (price, quality, overall offer) that are prevailing. For example, if a customer accounts for more than 25 per cent of turnover, they are able to move their custom and they think that they could get a better deal elsewhere, then they are in a powerful bargaining position.

Therefore, situations that can increase competition (and increase its significance) include:

- When the market is expanding or new, for example online auctions.
- When the stakes are high and there are major profits to be gained, notably when there are relatively few organisations in a large market (as with Cisco, Lucent or Intel).
- When the market is set to change, perhaps as a result of changes affecting patents and intellectual property rights, or as a result of political or legal developments (for example following the Microsoft anti-trust case).
- When the market is shrinking or when there is over-capacity in the market chasing fewer customers. This situation is apparent in manufacturing industries, although it has yet to make an impact on newer, technology-driven businesses of the 'new economy' (although that is not to say that it won't).

Understanding your competitors

There is a tendency for businesses either to dwell on their competitors' activities too much, spending an inordinate amount of time trying to second-guess developments, or else largely to ignore their competitors on the grounds that they are unable to exert any direct control. This is true of the offline, pre-Internet environment and largely in markets outside the USA. Clearly, the amount of attention that needs to be paid to competitors varies according to the nature of the industry and market, and is usually somewhere between the two extremes.

In certain industries or at certain times, it is necessary to focus intently on one's competitors. For example, if the launch of a major online development is planned, it is important to consider what is happening in the market and what your competitors are doing, before launching.

> **KEY CONCEPT**
>
> Very often, and to a significant extent, strategic direction is set by the decisions of individuals working at the middle level in organisations. Their decisions may be guided internally by the overall vision and their specific objectives, but external competitive pressures largely determine the choices they are presented with and the pressures they face.

Competitive issues

It is useful to develop a keen sense of market awareness, keeping up-to-date information about one's competitors and, in particular, how they are perceived in the market. Key issues to consider about competitors include the following:

- Pricing policies and the product offer as a whole.
- Customers' perceptions of your business; your main competitors; the market.
- Brand reputation and recognition – who is the market leader and why?
- Other external perceptions, including the views of journalists, markets and suppliers.

- Product quality.
- Service levels.
- Product portfolio.
- Organisation of competitors' businesses, notably their size, whether they enjoy economies of scale, the type of employees they attract, the amount they spend on training, their expenditure on product development, their distribution channels.
- The timing of promotional campaigns, whether they offer special promotions and the main sales channels used.
- Flexibility and organisational culture.
- Staff loyalty.
- Customer loyalty.
- Financial structure and cash reserves.

Maintaining an awareness of these issues will help to identify where direct competitors are strong, and where they are weak and open to competition. It can also help in analysing sources of competitive advantage.

Developing sources of competitive advantage

Factors commonly used to build competitive advantage online

The key to competing is clearly to have an expanding market share, so that ultimately the business can use its size to develop economies of scale, resulting in more customers being attracted and perpetuating a cycle of dominance. This cycle can be started – and, conversely, resisted – using the following factors.

Cash reserves can be used to finance sustained marketing campaigns, innovative development programmes or price reductions. They can also hold prices in the common event that escalating costs sweep the industry. *Purchasing power* is also important, as providing the ability to secure goods or services at a steady rate can help significantly in developing competitiveness. One popular approach is to build close working relations with preferred suppliers. In this way cost is not necessarily viewed as the only important factor; preferred suppliers will often ensure consistent quality, prices and delivery in return for an agreed level of business. The approach and organisation of the business, its *organisational culture*, need to suit the market. For example, if there is typically a high degree of staff turnover in the industry, the business needs to be geared up to recruiting the best employees. If flexibility and speed of response is valuable (and online it always is), the organisation needs to be able to anticipate major decisions, as well as to make the right choices and implement them.

Every organisation needs effective leadership, team building, processes and many other similar factors, but some are more important at certain times, in certain industries, than others. They can provide competitive advantage, or, perhaps more commonly, their absence can be a source of disadvantage. The business needs to be market focused and develop a keen sense of *market awareness*, understanding who its customers are and what they want (and do not want). Few markets are clearly defined and while a business may be open to any potential customer, it is important to know exactly who the core customers are, so that their interests can be given priority in the planning and running of the business. At times, this may even mean turning business away.

Finally, many of the factors that have the greatest impact on competitiveness relate directly to the *value proposition*, although they invariably inter-relate with the other factors mentioned above. Some of the most significant include pricing and discounts; distribution channels and availability; marketing methods; brand reputation and appeal; product quality; and how the product relates to others.

GETTING STARTED: developing resources and competitive advantage online

The take-off point for developing competitive advantage is to understand whether you wish to be in the market as a first mover/pioneer, an early adopter, a pioneer or an incumbent. (The merits and drawbacks of each are outlined in Chapter 8, Using the Internet for profitable product innovation.) It is also important to take this approach further, considering the specific differences between new entrants and incumbents in your business. In completing this review, there are five key principles for the online business to consider, which are enormously significant in determining competitiveness and profitability.

1 The Internet is the driver of change, not the change itself

When developing your online business it is important to throw away the rule book. The Internet enables so much radical change that would have been inconceivable in the past that the current path of the industry's development is usually – almost always – irrelevant. Certainly the approach of businesses as diverse as SAP and Amazon.com highlight the importance of using the strengths of the Internet to construct an entirely new and hugely popular value proposition. In the case of Amazon.com, its approach is based on the vision of its founder (and *Time* magazine's 1999 man of the year) Jeff Bezos that the online environment will grow and proliferate as a retailing medium. This approach is different to viewing the Internet as another business tool, no more significant, perhaps, than the development of the fax machine, telephone or spreadsheet. If the latter view is adopted the greatest challenge faced by the business is to put its brochure online. Clearly, this misses the power of the Internet to drive change where it matters most, in creating real value for the customer.

2   Competitive advantage online starts with customer focus

Looking for competitive advantage and profitability online means asking how the business can organise everything it does to serve customers more effectively. To achieve this, it can help to put yourself in the customer's position, perhaps even employing customers in your organisation (and using your own products, if possible). Every successful online business has two vital features in common: they focus all their effort on enhancing the customer's experience, and they constantly seek to improve and enhance that experience.

3   The profit-driven e-business must understand its strengths and weaknesses and act on them

For an established business (an incumbent) to succeed online it is necessary to do three things:

- It is important to understand what advantages the business has over its competitors and leverage these. This may include, for example, better relations with suppliers that enable the incumbent to compete more effectively on price or delivery lead time.
- Leaders need to understand where their business is weak, vulnerable or threatened and take action to remedy these problems. Most frequently this means developing a culture in the business of market awareness and continuous improvement, not easy changes to make in any business and certainly not an established one. Developing a senior-level e-commerce team to drive online developments may be an important step toward this.
- The online business needs to lead the market, unafraid to experiment in its on-going effort to maximise sales and build new sources of advantage that are difficult for competitors to replicate.

4 Whatever market position you have, competitors must be anticipated and countered

It is a fallacy to think that every move of a competitor needs to be anticipated or countered, but two factors are important to consider when competing:

♦ Understand how customers perceive competitors in two areas: their business brand in general and their value proposition in particular.

♦ Develop strategic resources (such as supply chains, customer bases, intellectual property, brand strength and awareness, people's skills and expertise) that provide barriers to entry for new competitors and sources of advantage relative to existing competitors.

5 Innovation, both in product and service quality, is essential because online no advantage is sustainable for long

The online environment changes so rapidly that no source of value or advantage lasts for long; the challenge is therefore to develop an online business capable of constantly adapting, continuously improving and creating superior sources of competitive advantage. This can be achieved by establishing:

♦ systems online and in the organisation structure to study and understand customer needs;

♦ measures for monitoring competitors;

♦ measures to assess customer trends – notably, how buying habits are altering;

♦ a business audit highlighting where the business needs to change and the capabilities and resources that it must develop;

♦ teams that are dynamically led and empowered to make key business decisions;

♦ methods for keeping up to date with technological developments.

The success of any strategy is relative. A strategy may be well conceived and executed, it may even succeed in achieving its aims, but if it is outmanoeuvred by its competitors the result is usually failure. Therefore it is essential to focus on the success of the strategy *relative* to other developments (among competitors and in the market or battlefield generally). Clearly, to be robust and successful a strategy needs to take account of competition: what competitors have done, are doing and may do in the future. In certain instances it can also be useful to consider the worst-case scenario: what would happen if . . .? In this way the strategy can be made more durable and realistic.

Online solutions: delivering profitability

CHAPTER 13

Overview

This chapter is designed as a summary, highlighting some of the key ideas and themes from the previous chapters and explaining how they can be implemented to drive profits for the online business. Focusing on strategies and leading-edge techniques to boost profits is fine, but the great advantages of the Internet are its ease and immediacy. Grand designs can deliver grand results, but more than ever, quick and easy techniques can deliver results out of all proportion to the effort required, and they can often be implemented five times a day if needed!

As the preceding chapters have demonstrated, there are many issues to consider when building a profitable online business. This chapter provides ideas and practical examples to boost profits today, and focuses on three issues that are decisive to achieving business success (as they have always been). They are:

CONTINUED ... **Overview**

- Customers and market innovations.
- People.
- Finance.

Success in these areas will help the online business quickly and easily to establish its credibility, building momentum and driving long-term flexibility and change.

Customers and market innovations

To be successful online requires a clear, unambiguous focus on customers, and in particular an approach that aims to improve perceived value in the customer–supplier relationship. Companies must establish seamless relationships with consumers or business customers that cover the whole of their business activities. Over the last five years, companies have developed a range of Internet practices that can have an impact at each phase of the value chain: from improving customers' buying process and decisions, to enhancing the quality of customer service and to rewarding and retaining loyal customers. Techniques for achieving these aims – and driving profits – are detailed below for each phase of customer acquisition, service and retention.

Techniques for improving customer service and satisfaction online

Focus on improving and speeding up product delivery times

An example of this is the efforts made by online retailers to ensure speedy deliveries, going so far as to give firm commitments for delivery times.

Improving value for the customer by providing details of price alternatives and best buys

The online environment brings with it much greater price transparency than ever before. If you tell your customers how much other sites are charging, unless you are very uncompetitive they will have no reason to leave your site to check other prices. Clearly, this will only work with specific customers, products and markets, but it may be worth considering. An example of this is certain banks and financial investment businesses, where competitor comparisons are normal.

Adding value by giving more for the same price

This is a tried and trusted approach, probably since people first started trading! On the Internet it can mean leveraging *content* and information, so that in addition to the product the customer buys they receive something else that has real value and benefit.

Confirming orders and/or knowing where you stand

One of the greatest fears many people still have about trading on the Internet is the anonymity of the process; once a decision has been reached and a purchase made, despite any number of acknowledgements customers still want to be able to follow their purchase. (Incidentally, this insecurity lies behind much of the legislation on data protection and freedom of information in the western world enacted during the last five years.) Dell and Federal Express are two organisations that have acted on this for their customers, investing in the issue so that it becomes a source of real competitive advantage.

Opening channels of communication for feedback and complaint handling

Many organisations have established feedback desks for their online customers, which can be turned to positive advantage if there are special offers that are provided regularly or if constant customer feedback is useful to the development process. However, it is also a source of competitive advantage in its own right, and businesses such as QVC have used it to strengthen their market appeal.

Focusing on individual customer needs and delivering these over time

Many businesses talk about the importance of customer needs: in practice, if you know what your customer wants – or might want – there is great advantage in simply offering it to them next time they come to your site. On-line food retailers are a clear example: you can choose your shopping and order it online, and next time you come to the site your previous choices and preferences are remembered and offered to you. This provides *convenience* (one of the ten critical drivers of success online) and can contribute to your customer's decision to return.

Techniques for improving sales

Providing information and education about products online

The Internet is distinguished both by its immediacy and complexity: anything that your site can do to increase the immediacy of your product proposition and reduce complexity is, usually, very welcome to customers. Web sites selling cars are a prime example. They are attractive and provide information in a direct, clear way; they also help the customer make a major purchase, both by providing information online but also by explaining what is available offline, from distributors.

Targeting one-on-one offers that suit particular needs

Customisation is another critical driver of commercial success online and in practice it can be achieved by tailoring product offers to individual customers. For example, on some news web sites it is possible to describe what information you wish to receive (e.g. sports and financial news) and have this sent regularly to your desktop. Customisation is not only a means of enhancing loyalty but also a way of increasing prices.

Improving convenience and reducing customer effort by remote purchasing

It is important to remember that competition for the online business comes not simply from other Internet traders but most of all from the offline world as well. Again, the issue of convenience is an important one to leverage here: the Internet is immediate and constantly accessible and this is often used as a source of competitive advantage. An example of this is home deliveries by many Internet grocery stores.

Adding to customers' choice while not having to carry the inventory

Not all of the techniques for improving customer satisfaction rely on additional expense: online booksellers are a prime example of sites that effectively act as brokers. They may not physically own the millions of books available on the site (as a conventional bookstore would have to), but they can offer the product and a reliable, competitive service nonetheless. This example also highlights the advantage of thinking innovatively by focusing on customers.

Reducing customers' concerns by showing products and allowing trial of downloads

The Internet gives the perfect opportunity for digital products to be downloaded and tried out, which is a useful way to remove customers' fears, uncertainties and doubts.

This approach can be extended to include more than merely digital products and services, driving additional traffic to the site in a way that helps significantly to reduce cost. Sample products also help customers to decide, and if this help and support is achieved on your web site then your customer will be much more likely to return and to tell others about it.

Techniques for rewarding customer loyalty online

Making special offers to targeted customers
It is worth remembering that the Internet is a mass medium, but much more significantly it is a personal, one-to-one medium as well. This can be leveraged to target groups of customers, or types of product, or any combination of the two. To achieve this, however, it is necessary to seek, collect and analyse customer data and ensure that your online business has the necessary features

> **KEY CONCEPT**
>
> Every successful online business has two features in common: they focus all their effort on enhancing the customer's experience, and they constantly seek to improve and enhance that experience.

for effective data mining. For special offers to work well and add value to the relationship, they do need to be genuinely valued by the customer – simply dumping excess products via the web site is far from satisfactory.

Creating exchange opportunities for customers
Many businesses offer their customers opportunities for exchanging products, ideas or information with other people. The facility to connect people and allow discussion is a unique benefit of the Internet and one that many businesses and their customers value. Perhaps two of the most obvious (and diverse) examples would be music fans brought together by a record company to exchange news, information and

comments; and doctors and medical clinicians brought together by pharmaceutical companies online, this practice raises the profile and authority of the company and adds value for its potential customers.

Creating new business opportunities for customers

Finally, if your business can help to create new commercial opportunities for your customers this will be rewarded with additional business, possibly even an additional business partner. In any event, creating commercial opportunities, while it may be difficult to accomplish, is a clear way to differentiate your online business and add significant value for your clients.

What is surprising about these Internet practices is how fast they have developed and moved from being competitive advantages for the companies that first employed them to being *competitive necessities* for companies using these capabilities today on the Internet.

People

Techniques for boosting the profitability of online activities include ensuring that there is a clear focus on people. One popular and effective idea to consider is *recruiting an e-business expert*, someone with experience who can take a fresh perspective on all aspects of your e-business activities. This may not need to be a permanent appointment and there are many consultancies that can provide this type of input, although it may be quicker, easier and more beneficial to appoint an individual who can fit within the organisation structure. The success of this idea, however, relies on the stage of development reached by the e-business: clearly, it is best suited to the organisation that is about to start a new phase of e-business activity.

Another people-oriented factor that is critical to achieving online success is *reviewing the organisation structure*. The business leader needs to ensure that the structure is flexible, flat and empowered enough to take advantage of business opportunities that may arise. *Training and development in e-skills* is fundamental and it is surprising how quickly this can have an impact on profitability. Nevertheless, personal professional development needs to be dynamic and on-going. Attracting and retaining experienced, e-business talent is another source of competitive advantage and profit. It is certainly worth *reviewing remuneration for key staff* and paying them according to their market value and worth. Measures for *active knowledge and information sharing* can also provide enormous and decisive benefit to the online business.

Finance

There are several key areas where focused financial management can boost profits and many other areas that are specific to each business. This finance section concludes with some questions designed to help you uncover the areas where you can boost profits through better financial management for your e-business, but it starts by focusing on the 'generic' key areas for profit boosting:

- Improving the efficiency of accounts receivable.
- Reducing the costs of inventory.
- Utilising capacity.
- Understanding and developing your financial information requirements.

Improving the efficiency of accounts receivable

Accounts receivable carry an associated cost to finance them, the administrative costs of processing them and the risks associated with not collecting them. Most companies take this as a given, yet in the online environment they are often overlooked (or overpowered) by a focus on the customer that screams for market share and customer loyalty, at the expense of prudent financial management. It is vital to keep in mind the simple truth that processing repeated bills to delinquent customers adds to their overall costs. As with costs associated with servicing different customers to varying degrees, differences in payment and collection can add a further element of profit or loss distinction to customer categories and specific customers.

Reducing the costs of inventory

The cost of carrying inventory is often higher than one thinks and may be the difference between profitable and unprofitable products and customers. In addition to the financial costs associated with carrying inventory, there are people and facility costs associated with storage and moving, the risk of obsolescence and damage, insurance and taxes, and many other associated costs. This high cost, coupled with slow inventory turns, can have a significant, implicit impact on profit margins.

> **KEY CONCEPT**
>
> It is not unusual for manufacturing companies to have inventory carrying costs in the order of 25–30 per cent of the value of the product. If the issue of inventory is not addressed and very carefully managed, then the pressures for online trading – and the need to deliver fast and reliably – can destroy any hope of profitability in an explosion of direct and indirect expenses.
>
> One of the keys to success, both online and offline, is to ensure that stock is turned frequently.

Using the Internet – or more precisely, customer information derived from the Internet – is a valuable way of delivering faster inventory turns and lower costs of carrying inventory reduce its economic impact.

Utilising capacity

Property and plant are affected by improvements in material management. If a company increases its inventory turns from three times to ten times, it has reduced its inventory by two-thirds. Many online businesses are moving to becoming 'virtual businesses'; even for traditional companies, the space savings resulting from information-driven efficiencies and outsourcing can be very important, but are frequently overlooked. For example, the implications of space savings resulting from better, just-in-time management of inventory are reductions in investment cost, depreciation expense, on-going maintenance and other related costs.

Understanding and developing your financial information requirements

As the issue of capacity utilisation highlights, effective financial analysis derives its potential value from a good information system. Fortunately, the online environment provides many opportunities for effectively constructing and integrating financial management systems. However, if a good information system does not exist, or it is flawed, the likelihood is that the benefits will fall short of what could result had there been better information.

 IMPLEMENTATION CHECKLIST: finding areas for reducing costs and boosting profits within your business

The following ideas clearly overlap and are not intended to provide a sequential process for reducing costs and boosting profits. Rather, they are intended to provide a thought-provoking guide to the main areas of cost control and profit maximisation.

Assessing, monitoring and managing profitability

1　Do you have the resources and processes in place to monitor the effect of online activities on revenue, cost and profit? Have you, for example, considered establishing (or updating) key performance indicators (KPIs) that assess how areas as wide-ranging as repeat business and production lead times are affected by online activities?

2　Does the business put as much emphasis on asset management as it does on cost management and reduction? For example:

- Has the company calculated the full cost of carrying an extra day of accounts receivable?
- Has the company calculated the aggregate full cost of carrying inventories? What does this represent on a unit cost basis?
- Does the company have in place a programme explicitly to reduce the amount of property, plant and equipment it utilises? What results can it show from its efforts?

Cost allocations and profitability analysis

3　Has the business re-analysed its overhead cost assignments to products in the past five years?

4　Does the business use appropriate assessments of overhead cost drivers (or are these too broad or simply outdated and irrelevant)?

5　Has the business assigned its non-manufacturing operating expenses to its various markets, channels and customers so that customer profitability can be monitored accurately?

6　Has the business made any attempt to assign working capital and fixed assets to products and customers, as appropriate?

Customers and products

7 Are customers' needs central? Do they influence what is made and when?

8 Can the business rank order its customers by profitability, including the accurate and beneficial assignment of all costs to those customers (see point 5)?

9 Is there a formal process for gathering customers' wants, needs and their willingness to pay for functionality?

10 Is there a similar process for gathering competitive product and cost information? Is there an attempt to ascertain competitors' future product/cost intentions?

11 Could the business initiate a target cost planning process, replacing a more traditional 'cost plus' methodology?

12 Has the percentage of costs that may be directly assigned to products increased? Can the business calculate the change?

13 What proportion of cost management time and cost is devoted to the design stages, as against prototype and production stages?

14 Who is involved in the product planning process? Is it a cross-functional team?

15 Have the business's underlying cost systems been modified to provide a foundation for product cost planning?

Eliminating waste (predominantly in manufacturing businesses)

16 Has the business applied process analysis thinking to its manufacturing operations or to its non-manufacturing activities?

17 Has the business initiated waste identification and elimination initiatives? For example, has a set-up time reduction programme been put in place? Is it within or outside manufacturing?

18 Does the business really know its inventory carrying costs? Are there programmes in place to reduce these costs?

Establishing a culture of profit maximisation and continuous improvement

19 Is there a culture of cost awareness, control and reduction prevailing in your organisation? Does it influence management action? If not, how might profitable behaviour (as distinct from revenue-generating behaviour) be incentivised?

20 Has the business considered reassigning indirect, support personnel to more direct activities?

21 Has the company broadened job classifications to provide for greater responsibilities? Have spans of control been widened and have the number of levels in the organisation been reduced?

22 Have costs been reduced as the result of an explicit effort to flatten the organisation? By how much?

23 Has the company made continuous cost improvement an integral part of its corporate culture? What examples demonstrate this and what lessons can be learned?

24 What role does senior management play in implementing cost-reduction initiatives?

25 Are there techniques in place such as Pareto analysis and root cause analysis to monitor cost-reduction accomplishments? Who has responsibility for this and how is the information shared?

Value chain analysis

26 What proportion of the business's costs are represented by purchased materials and supplies? Does the business focus a comparable level of cost management attention on this category?

27 How well does the organisation understand the root cause of suppliers' prices, on an on-going basis? What attempt is made to reduce them and how?

28 How well equipped is the business to standardise and simplify products and services, where appropriate?

29 Has the business considered partnering with vendors (suppliers)? How could this be achieved, what might be the benefits – and where are the risks?

30 Has the business reviewed its extended value chain, assessing who makes money, who does not, and how?

31 Has the business considered its own internal value chain? Where along the chain does the business add unique value? Where is value not added and where is it dissipated?

32 Has the business undertaken an analysis of those activities that it might outsource?

1   Downes, L. and Mui, C. (1998) *Unleashing the Killer App*, Boston, MA: Harvard Business School Press.

2   Source: data based on information from The Economist Intelligence Unit (EIU) and other sources. (For further information see the report *Competing in the Digital Age – how the Internet will transform global business*, published by the EIU with Booz Allen Hamilton, New York, 1999. Additional data and analysis is available at EIU.com, and is also contained in *E-Business Transformation*, published by The EIU in cooperation with IBM Global Services, New York, 2000, and *Business, People and Rewards – surviving and thriving in the new economy*, published by the EIU in cooperation with Towers Perrin, New York, 2001.)

3   For a closer examination of the power of extranets, intranets and other network capabilities, see Professor Donald Marchand's excellent book *Competing with Information*, Chichester: Wiley, 2000. Chapter 17, Building e-commerce capabilities: the four-net challenge, is especially relevant for the business focusing on meeting networking challenges.

4   There are two classic texts about leadership during a time of change that are as relevant to the environment of e-commerce and rapid technological and market change as they were when they were first written. *Leading Change* (John Kotter, Boston, MA: Harvard Business School Press, 1996) is one and *The Art of Strategy* (London: HarperCollins, 1988), originally written by Sun Tzu over 2000 years ago, is the other.

5   Interestingly, variations of these five stages have been used in several publications, both online and offline. However, the most impressive and original outline is from *Customers.com: How to Create a Profitable Business Strategy for the Internet* (Patricia B. Seybold with Ronni T. Marshak, New York: Random House Business Books, 1999). It is important that the five stages are viewed as an improvement cycle, with each stage directly enhancing the next so that, for example, a strong sense of community (stage 5) enables company and product information to be provided more effectively (stage 1).

Attwood, Ray (1998) 'The young pretenders', *Supply Management*, 3(20, 8 Oct.): 22–4.

Barclays Bank (1996) *Using the Internet as a Business Tool*, London: Barclays.

Barrow, Colin (2000) 'Phasing the facts', *Director*, 54(2, Sept.): 76–80.

Bonnett, Kendra (2000) *The IBM Guide to Doing Business on the Internet*, New York, NY: McGraw-Hill.

Boynton, Andrew and Pukrand, James (2000) 'E-business and your company: lessons from Silicon Valley', *Perspectives for Managers* supplement, May.

Brache, Alan and Webb, Jim (2000) 'The eight deadly assumptions of e-business', *Journal of Business Strategy*, 21(2, May/June): 13–17.

Carter, Meg (2000) 'Cyber house rules', *People Management*, 6(13, 23 June): 28–36.

Centre for Strategic Business Studies (2000) *E-commerce: Challenge and Opportunity*, Winchester: CSBS Publications.

Corboy, Martin (1999) 'E-commerce: dispelling the myths and exploiting the opportunities', *Management Accounting*, 77(11, Dec.): 38–42.

Cornet, Paul, Milcent, Paul and Roussel, Pierre Yves (2000) 'From e-commerce to euro-commerce', *McKinsey Quarterly* supplement, 2: 31–8.

Crush, Peter (2000) 'No place for wimps', *Human Resources UK*, June: 28–31.

Downton, Steve (2000) 'E-business in service', *Control UK*, 26(6, July/Aug.): 18–20.

Duffy, Jan (2000) 'Point of no return beyond e-commerce: the customer-centric e-business', *CMA Management*, 74(2, Mar.): 32–7.

Dussart, Christian (2000) 'Internet: the one plus eight revolutions', *European Management Journal*, 18(4): 386–97.

Dutta, Soumitra and Segev, Arie (1999) 'Business transformation on the Internet', *European Management Journal*, 17(5, Oct.): 466–76.

Dutta, Soumitra, Kwan, Stephen and Segev, Arie (1998) 'Business transformation in electronic commerce: a study of sectoral and regional trends', *European Management Journal*, 16(5, Oct.): 540–51.

Earl, Michael J. (2000) 'Evolving the e-business', *Business Strategy Review*, 11(2, Summer): 33–8.

Eglash, Joanne (2000) *How to Write a .com Business Plan: the Internet*

Entrepreneur's Guide to Everything You Need to Know About Business Plans and Financing Options, New York, NY: McGraw-Hill.

Ghosh, Shikhar (1998) 'Making business sense of the Internet', *Harvard Business Review*, 76(2, Mar./Apr.): 126–35.

Goldberg, Beverly and Sifonis, John G. (1998) 'Focusing your E-commerce vision', *Management Review*, Sept.: 48–51.

Gornall, Jonathan (1998) 'Cyberspace unravelled', *Director*, 53(3, Oct.): 80–91.

Griffith, David A. and Palmer, Jonathan W. (1999) 'Leveraging the web for corporate success', *Business Horizons*, 42(1, Jan./Feb.): 3–10.

Hall, Jeff (2000) 'Are your processes fit for ecommerce?', *Management Services*, 44(4, Apr.): 12–16.

Hamel, Gary and Sampler, Jeff (1998) 'The ecorporation: more than just web based, it's building a new industrial order', *Fortune International*, 138(11, 7 Dec.): 52–63.

Houlder, Vanessa (1998) 'Fear and enterprise as the net closes in', *Financial Times*, 20 May: 18.

Hutchinson, Malcolm (1998) 'E-commerce set to explode', *Management NZ*, 45(9, Oct.): 61–7.

Kakabadse, Nada K., Kouzmin, Alexander and Kakabadse, Andrew K. (2000) 'Current trends in Internet use: e-communication, e-information and e-commerce', *Knowledge and Process Management*, 7(3): 133–42.

King, David (1999) 'The development of UK home food shopping', *Logistics and Transport Focus*, 1(6, Dec.): 18–27.

Lynn, Matthew (2000) 'Mice in the body shop', *Management Today*, Aug.: 54–7.

MacLeod, Marcia (2000) 'Talk about a revolution', *Supply Management*, 5(1, Jan): 28–9.

Mahadevan, B. (2000) 'Business models for internet-based e-commerce: an anatomy', *California Management Review*, 42(4, Summer): 55–69.

May, Paul (2000) *The Business of E-commerce: From Corporate Strategy to Technology*, Breakthroughs in Application Development series, Cambridge: Cambridge University Press.

McGettrick, Brendan, Bell, Scott and Green, Pat (2000) 'E-business or no business: strategies for continuous growth', *Control UK*, 26(5 June): 17–20.

Net Profit (2000) 'What do we get in exchange?', *Net Profit*, 46(Oct.): 10–11.

Norris, Mark, West, Steve and Gaughan, Kevin (2000) *E-business Essentials: Technology and Network Requirements for the Electronic Marketplace*, BT series, Chichester: Wiley.

Parker, David (2000) 'The future's not what it used to be', *Management Services*, 44(12, Dec.): 16–17.

Pensera, Joseph J. (1999) 'E-commerce economics and regulation', *SAM Advanced Management Journal*, 64(4, Autumn): 39–47.

Plant, Robert (1999) 'Crafting a coherent internet strategy', *Financial Times*, Mastering Management.

Rock, Stuart (ed.) (2000) *Making eBusiness Deliver*, London: Caspian Publishing.

Roth, Daniel (1999) 'My what big Internet numbers you have', *Fortune International*, 139(5, 15 Mar.): 48–52.

Rowley, Jennifer (2000) 'Coupling e-business with knowledge management', *Managing Information*, 7(5, June): 59–62.

Segars, Albert (2000) 'The seven myths of e-commerce', *Financial Times*, Mastering Management.

Singleton, Susan and Simon Halberstam (1999) *Business, the Internet and the Law: a Practical Guide*, Croydon: Tolley.

Small Business Research Trust (2000) *E-commerce*, Quarterly Small Business Management Report, Milton Keynes: Lloyds TSB.

Suff, Paul (2000) *E-commerce*, London: Eclipse.

Supply Management (2000) 'Guide to e-procurement', *Supply Management* supplement 5(19, 21 Sept.): 1–30.

Timmers, Paul (1999) *Electronic Commerce: Strategies and Models for Business-to-Business Trading*, Chichester: Wiley.

Tyler, Geoff (2000) 'Taking centre stage', *Supply Management*, 5(17, 24 Aug.): 24–8.

Voss, Chris (2000) 'Developing an e-service strategy', *Business Strategy Review*, 11(1, Spring): 21–33.

Watson, Richard T., Berthon, Pierre, Pitt, Leyland and Zinkhon, George (2000) *Electronic Commerce: the Strategic Perspective*, Fort Worth, TX: Dryden Press.

Watts, Julian (2000) 'Riding the wave', *Supply Management*, 5(19, 21 Sept.): 26–30.

William, Ruth L. and Cothrel, Joseph (2000) 'Four smart ways to run online communities', *Sloan Management Review*, 41(4, Summer): 81–91.

Zott, Christoph, Amit, Raphael and Donlevy, Jon (2000) 'Strategies for value creation in e-commerce: best practice in Europe', *European Management Journal*, 18(5, Oct.): 463–75.

INDEX

interactions, concepts 13, 31–6,
  61, 83–91, 117, 222–3,
  235–6
intermediaries, information
  187–9
Internet xi–xiv, 1–14, 224–32
  see also web sites
  24/7 concepts 5, 30, 113, 121
  advertising techniques 2–3,
    18, 45, 82–91, 118,
    126–7, 158–64
  assessments 15–23, 36–9,
    60–1, 81–5, 113–17,
    156–7, 243
  change driver attributes 229
  developments 57–64, 116,
    122–6, 203–18, 229–32
  education requirements
    49–50, 54–7
  feasibility issues 18–23, 168
  information management
    186–99
  knowledge management
    186–99
  leadership issues 48–69
  learning cycles 8–10, 155
  market segmentation
    concepts 72–83, 145–6,
    160–1
  pricing methods 7, 38–9, 45,
    93–107, 235
  ten critical drivers of e-
    commerce 13–14,
    23–46, 150–2, 236
  time issues 5–6, 80, 95, 112,
    161
Internet service providers
  (ISPs), partnerships 58–9,
  128
intimacy factors 73
intranets 38
Intuit 12
inventory costs 205, 237, 241,
  243–5
invitations to tender 176–7
IPR *see* intellectual property
  rights
ISPs *see* Internet service
  providers
iVillage.com 32

JIT *see* just in time
Jungle 75
just in time (JIT) 207

kaizen 212
  see also continuous
    improvements
Kermally, Sultan 199
key performance indicators
  (KPIs) 215, 217–18, 243

knowledge 2, 165–6, 183–99
  see also information
  audits 190–1
  case studies 8–10
  concepts 7–10, 183–99
  decision making 16, 85–6,
    184–99
  increases 190–1
  leverage issues 7–10, 123,
    219
  maintenance processes 191
  management 183–99,
    243–6
  overview 183–4
  pitfalls 193–4
  profits 183–99
  tacit knowledge 84, 191–2
  types 84, 191–2
KPIs *see* key performance
  indicators

leadership issues 47–69, 161–6
  changes 48–57
  communication
    requirements 52–3, 55,
    67, 68–9
  concepts 48–69, 120–1, 161,
    240
  confidence requirements
    51–2, 55, 193–4
  culture 54–7, 194, 228, 245
  education requirements
    49–50, 54–7
  empowerment needs 48, 53,
    55–7, 68, 120–1
  momentum processes 53–4
  overview 47–8
  performance standards
    62–3, 169–71, 175–6,
    217–18
  pitfalls 57, 65
  remoteness problems 56–7
  vision 52–3, 55, 61–2,
    174–6, 229
  vital empowerment
    questions 55–7
learning cycles 8–10, 155–6
legal issues 18, 166, 192, 194
leverage issues 7–10, 123, 219,
  235
linked web sites 35–6
loss leading strategies 99
loyalty issues 4–7, 14, 35, 45,
  61, 73, 79
  concepts 85–7, 105, 115–16,
    130–48, 227, 238–9
  human resources 45, 48, 227
  implementation checklist
    137–41
  overview 129–30
  profits 133–41, 238–9

marginal cost pricing strategies
  101–2
market research uses 104–5,
  154–5
market sensing uses 104–5
market shares 7, 121, 227–32
marketing 18, 104–7, 118, 132,
  137–41
markets 10–12, 64, 66, 104–7
  see also competition . . .
  awareness factors 44–5,
    62–3, 75–6, 228–32
  cannibalisation practices
    42–3
  concepts 71–91, 110–15,
    154–60
  cycle of dominance concepts
    227–8
  developments 71–91
  entry positions 162–4, 224
  first-movers 161, 162–4, 229
  identification needs 19–27,
    39–40, 66–7, 85–6,
    154–60, 206, 230–9,
    244
  new entrants 161–4, 224,
    229–32
  overview 71
  Porter's five forces 224–5
  positioning concepts
    158–64
  segmentation concepts 4–5,
    60, 72–83, 145–6,
    160–1
  trends 3–5, 44, 85–6, 155,
    231
  vital questions 104–7
Metcalf's Law 13
Microsoft Windows 8
milking strategies 100
momentum processes 53–4
monitoring benefits 88–90, 94,
  132, 198–9, 217–18, 231,
  243

navigation requirements 33–4,
  122–5
networking benefits 31–2, 196
  see also communications
*New Economy Energy:
  Unleashing Knowledge for
  Competitive Advantage*
  (Kermally) 199
new entrants, markets 161–4,
  224, 229–32
new products 85–6, 117–18,
  135, 149–66

objectives 10–12, 65–6, 106–7,
  131–2, 176–7
online business concepts 1–14